Whimberries on the Coity

GARN-YR-ERW IN THE 1940s

Elvina Hill

For my children and grandchildren

I am indebted to my uncle, aunts and cousins for delightful conversations of reminiscence.

For patience, encouragement and electronic assistance, I am grateful to Bill, my husband.

ISBN 978-1-905967-33-9

Published in the U.K. by
Old Bakehouse Publications
Church Street, Abertillery, Gwent NP13 1EA
Telephone: 01495 212600 Fax: 01495 216222
Email: theoldbakeprint@btconnect.com
www: oldbakehouseprint.co.uk

Made and printed in the UK
by J.R. Davies (Printers) Ltd.

British Library Cataloguing in Publication Data: a catalogue
record for this book is available from the British Library.

Contents

Vincent and Elsie Hill with Elvina and David 1940.

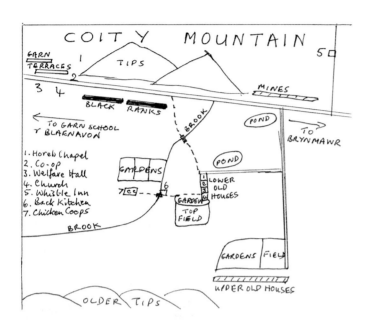

COITY MOUNTAIN

5□

GARN TERRACES

TIPS

1
2
3 4

MINES

BLACK RANKS

BROOK

POND

TO GARN SCHOOL
Y BLAENAVON

TO BRYNMAWR

1. Horeb Chapel
2. Co-op
3. Welfare Hall
4. Church
5. Whistle Inn
6. Back Kitchen
7. Chicken Coops

GARDENS

POND

1
2
3
4
LOWER OLD HOUSES

7 ☐
6
GARDEN

TOP FIELD

BROOK

GARDENS | FIELD

UPPER OLD HOUSES

OLDER TIPS

Garn-yr-erw 1940s showing slag heaps and Lower Old Houses right foreground.

4

Letter from the Middle East   15-9-1943

My Own Darling Elsie,

* * * * * * * *

The endless days and nights with no change at all make me feel I cannot wait much longer for you, darling, and all that I hold dear. I go over and over in my mind day after day our happy times together and try to get comfort from my sweet and golden memories. It's hard sometimes to keep that smile but keep it I must until that wonderful day arrives when it will broaden into a bigger smile still.

It's now nearly midnight with a cold breeze blowing across the sands after a burning hot day. I'm on duty tonight as Orderly Sergeant, a duty one has to perform with one's other work. The moon is full and it seems almost as bright as day. There is a sad stillness about with only the bark of a dog or the challenge of a sentry to break the silence, but there is something lovely about it and a wonderful contrast to the noise of guns and battle as it was a short while ago.

Father in Middle East 1943.

Well, my precious one, I hope all at home are well. All my love to you sweet and give my Nibs a big hug for me, and oh how I miss you all. Keep your chin up and I'll be coming along soon.

Your ever loving and devoted husband,
Vin

5

Chapter One
Arrival in Garn-yr-Erw

As the Spitfires roared overhead, I was hoisted aloft on somebody's shoulder. *'Wave!'* they cried, *'Wave! They're our boys going over!'* So we waved and waved until they were specks in the distance, and then no more. Soon after that my mother packed our bags, shut up the house by the sea, bade farewell to the Solleys next door, and took my brother and me to live with her family in Wales.

A steam train took us all the way from Brighton to Newport, a journey of five hours. There we boarded the red and yellow Ralph's bus which trundled and laboured its way up the narrow winding valley roads, ducking under low bridges, passing through numerous villages, scattering cackling geese and straggly sheep in all directions, ominously slipping backwards on steep hills while the intrepid driver manoeuvred a double de-clutch, and the passengers who hadn't fainted held suspended breath, until the labouring monster gradually edged its way forward, onward and upwards. After what seemed an eternity, we arrived in Garn-yr-erw. To an outsider, I suppose, it must have seemed a bleak and unlovely place, ravaged by the satanic machinery of coal-mining, dominated by one enormous black slag heap with a second fast growing, and a row of gloomy black houses lining the road. But I was too young to notice such things and from the first knew it only as a place where we were enveloped in thick blankets of warmth and love, a place where we belonged, in spite of joining that category of displaced war-time persons known as evacuees.

Nan and Granch seated with Arthur, Glad, Doll and Marion.

So we settled into the small whitewashed stone cottage, further up the mountain, where my grandparents had raised four girls and one boy. It was early 1941, fifteen months after the outbreak of World War Two; I was three years old and my brother two. My father had been called up, drafted into the armed forces along with all other able-bodied men between the ages of 18 and 41. From December 1940 until July 1942 he was stationed in Hampshire. We seldom saw him during this time since he could only visit on a seven-day leave. When he was granted forty-eight hours he could travel to Brighton, if funds allowed, to see his mother and sister, and occasionally his brothers. If time permitted he would also pop over to Hove to see friends and people at the hotel where he had worked. He was reluctant to visit our home when we were not there, however, as he found it too upsetting, but it gave him peace of mind that we were in Wales, safe from the air raids.

A neighbour by the Old Houses.

His final leave was in July 1942 when he was able to attend the Sunday School Anniversary at the Garn chapel. He was granted this one short leave before being packed on a troop ship, destined we knew not where, to fight for king and country in some foreign land. My Mother did not know if she would ever see him again. But his memory was kept alive by airmail letters and drawings, and by my mother who talked to us about him continually and kept up her own spirits by reviving ours.

Nan's cottage was No. 3 in a row of four nestling into the lower slope of the hillside and close by the brook. A small entrance porch, with a thick heavy door and an outer stable door, served as a scullery. Another heavy door, wedged open all day long by a smooth round polished lump of coal, led into the kitchen-cum-living room with its heavily beamed

Garn Landscape.

cream-painted ceiling and black range fireplace. Two doors, one at each end of the back wall, led to my grandparents' bedroom and the pantry respectively, while another door set into the wall by the fireplace opened to reveal a short flight of stairs leading to two upper bedrooms. The one at the top of the stairs had a skylight while the inner room had a small deep window seat (the outer walls of the cottage being two feet thick) looking out over the path leading to the brook, and then away over to the mountains and tips. There was electricity and running water but no bathroom.

My new world was bounded by the long range of the Coity Mountain, its scarp slope rising up like a mighty wall between our valley and the next. It held a magical fascination for me.

'Granch,' I said one day, *'if I stood on top of the Coity with a long pole, could I touch the sky? '*

'No, my lovely, for the higher you are, the higher the sky. It's way, way above even the mighty Coity. But when you are a little bit older and your legs are stronger we shall climb the Coity together and you shall try to reach the sky.'

So the Coity mountain with its ever descending mists and the cloud shadows which played across its surface remained a mystery for the present time.

Between the road and the Coity were two huge black tips, man-made from the waste of the Kay-Slope Colliery where the majority of men on the Garn hacked out their twilight lives. I was fascinated by the little trolley which ran up the side of the tip on a rail-track. On reaching the top it would empty out its load which came crashing and rumbling down to settle amongst the slack. The tipping of the slack was a perpetual background noise to our daily lives. Sometimes, I would stand mesmerised for ages, watching this rhythmical mechanised performance. An acrid, pervasive smell of smouldering rubble permanently hung over the valley.

In front of the tips and parallel with the Coity ran the ribbon of a road as far as the eye could see: up to Brynmawr one way and down to Blaenavon the other. Fair View and Fair Mount, the Black Rank houses, lined one side of the road. These houses were white when they were built, but when they started to let in the damp the Coal Board waterproofed them with tar-based black paint to avoid any repair bills. Hideous on the outside, many were comfortably furnished inside and several boasted a front parlour which was used only on special occasions. Beyond these lay the tiny church, the welfare hall, and the bungalow, the only decent-looking house on the Garn, where Uncle Jack and Auntie Sarah lived with their invalid daughter, Margaret. Opposite the church was the Co-op (pronounced *'Cworperaytive'*), the most unprepossessing of all unprepossessing Co-ops of that time, and nearby were two rows of stone

cottages, Upper and Lower Garn Terrace. A short distance down behind the Co-op lay the Horeb Chapel.

Nan's row of houses was up on the hillside (though we called it the mountain), some distance from the roadway, reached by a footpath and a bridge over the brook. For horse and cart and motorised vehicles there was a cinder track which also led further up the mountain to a terrace of nine small houses nudging older tips, evidence of former mine workings, whose sides and flattened tops sprouted tufts of grass, a valiant effort by nature to reclaim her own. One or two white-washed farms were scattered over the lower slopes of the Coity, near the Whistle Inn. Hardy grey sheep and wild ponies roamed everywhere.

It was indeed a bleak and barren landscape, but with one exception. Two huge elm trees stood in the walled front garden of top house, close by the brook. They dominated

Nan on the 'mountain' 1941.

the small cottages and echoed every nuance of the weather: waving their branches of rustling leaves in the gentle streams of air; sighing with branches waving as the wind rose; and then thrashing furiously as stormy gusts roared through them and fierce rain lashed down upon us all. Many a night I would curl up in the bedroom window-seat and watch this battle royal between the enraged heavens and the sturdy elms before sliding into bed and drifting into cosy sleep.

Granch 1941.

In Hove, my mother had grown used to a house with a bathroom. Now she had to readjust to more primitive arrangements: a tin bath filled from pots boiled up on the fire, and a lavatory down by the brook, which was scrubbed by Nan from floor to ceiling every Monday morning. The washing was done in a stone outhouse by the brook known as the back-kitchen which also doubled as Grancher's workshop. This housed some very interesting tools which David and I played with when the grown-ups weren't around. I loved winding up the vice, even though I often caught my fingers in it, as I did on the big mangle.

On washing days the back-kitchen became a steaming hothouse of lathery suds. First a huge fire was stoked up to heat gallons of water for boiling up the wash, and then all the clothes were placed in the big copper. Nan, wearing an overall and a beret with all her hair tucked inside, poked the clothes around in the boiler with a wooden dolly until they were cleaned to her satisfaction. Then they were hauled out, steaming like a dragon, and passed through the mangle. After being rinsed and mangled a second time they were taken up onto the mountain on the far side of the brook to be pegged on wire clothes lines. It was a source of great satisfaction to Nan when the wind was strong. *'I do love to see the clothes blowing on the line,'* she would say.

Every Saturday after tea the tin bath was placed in front of the fire, filled with warm water and then David and I were soaked and scrubbed. Afterwards, in clean pyjamas, we would invent daft games like *'See who can lean furthest back over the bath without falling in'* while Mam and Nan were otherwise occupied. The game developed into a fierce competition until David, determined to outdo me, leant back a bit too far and fell right in with a mighty splash which sent water flying in all directions, dousing the fire and soaking the chairs and

*Elvina and David in
Grancher's garden.*

rugs. My mother's quick temper was up in a flash and she threatened to beat us both. I fled up the stairs terrified and left David to his fate.

Another Saturday night ritual, and one which I loathed, was the routine dose of California Syrup of Figs. After scrubbing on the outside, an attempt was made to scour us on the inside with the idea, I suppose, we were then one hundred per cent clean for Chapel on Sunday. I am sure my grandparents must have longed for peace, not only from the war but also from the invasion of their grandchildren. Often after we had been put to bed at night and firmly told to go to sleep we would start singing songs we had heard on the wireless such as Macnamara's Band, John Brown's Body, Old Macdonald Had a Farm, Deep in the Heart of Texas and She'll be Coming Round the Mountain, getting louder and louder until we were threatened with a smack. Granch was once asked to look after us and in desperation he offered us sixpence each to be good, but we both said no thank you we would rather be naughty, or so the story goes.

Even this little village tucked away in the mountains was subject to wartime restrictions and regulations. The blackout was strictly enforced: there was no street lighting and all windows, already reinforced by criss-cross tape to protect the glass, had to be completely covered with blackout material before electric lights were switched on. ARP wardens did their rounds searching for recalcitrant chinks of light which might guide enemy aircraft. Coming home one dark moonless night, someone struck a match to check we were on the road - and found we were all walking into the pond.

Grancher was a member of the Home Guard, and the nights when he was on duty were quite a performance with all the rubbing, polishing, brassoeing (of brass buttons using a special gadget, a soldier's button stick, which fitted round the buttons and protected the khaki uniform from Brasso), and the blancoing of puttees. He would huff and puff as he pulled on various bits of uniform, drawing in his breath through his teeth with a hissing sound while Nan danced in attendance. *'Mother, have you seen my spare collar?'* or *'Mother, can you fix this stud for me?'* or *'Mother, where have you put the shoe horn?'* At last he would be ready with his rifle over his shoulder, and even the house breathed a sigh of relief as he left for duty.

Then Nan would say, *'Well, Else, my girl, we do need a cup of tea after that.'* Tea was on ration like almost everything else but we always seemed to have enough. However, a consequence of food rationing was that we were urged to eat bread and butter (or marg) with everything, including the fruit and custard that was standard fare for Sunday tea. For me, this ruined the delicious sharpness of the juicy fruit, usually plums, but I was never allowed one without the other. I loved Sunday breakfast, though, when we had bacon and eggs and sometimes tinned tomatoes. Eggs were scarce in general but we had plenty as my Aunty Glad, who also lived with us, kept chickens. I can still recall the wet-sawdust smell of the chicken feed being heated up in a great pail on the open fire, and the thrill of helping to scatter it amongst the strutting hens who would all come running and clucking, pushing their sisters out of the way as the food appeared. They had their scratching ground on the far side of the brook with the coops behind them.

Chickens were harmless but geese were the bane of my life. To be confronted by Mrs. Snook's gaggle of geese in the narrow lane, honking and blocking your path was a terrifying experience. Fat and white, with vicious yellow beaks and beady hostile eyes, they waddled towards you on webbed orange flappers. They could run, too, and stretch out their necks in an alarming manner while the honking and cackling gave way to a menacing hiss. At this point I always turned and fled, and of course they chased me, whereas Nan said you should stand your ground and shoo them away - something I could never do. Eventually Mr Snook sold the geese and bought a car (the first on the Garn) which solved my problem.

My grandfather had three gardens and a field in those days. The kitchen garden was a tiny plot beside the back-kitchen, where he grew flowers and herbs. Vegetables were grown in the larger garden on the far side of the brook. The furthest away was the top garden with its adjoining field, surrounded by dry stone walling. This bore sour gooseberries and rhubarb whose forbidden delights were the cause of many a stomach ache. Our craving for sweet things was satisfied by parcels from Mrs Solley, our former neighbour in Hove. For some unfathomable reason she had moved her family to London and the blitz while everyone else was seeking the relative safety of remote areas. On birthdays she always arrived in person, her suitcase loaded with candies, sticks of liquorice and iced cakes. My father commented in a letter: Mrs Solley is certainly a marvel to arrange such lovely eats for the party.

These were times of delight, but I also remember being ill quite often in those early years. My father sometimes mentioned these illnesses in his letters. In one (7-4-43, an answer to an airmail which he received six months after it was posted), he says: *'You tell me about Elvina being so poorly and how she said that if her Daddy was home she would soon be better.'* When the fever raged I felt my whole body disintegrate into thousands of tiny fragments which floated away across the bed. Cold flannels were pressed to my head to lower the temperature, and as the fever subsided the scattered fragments of my body would gradually come together again. Holding onto the cool brass rails of the bedstead also brought some comfort. As I began the long slow recovery my mother would a wrap shawl round both of us, Welsh style, and carry me around outside for short periods to enjoy a little sunshine and fresh air. These bouts of illness always began with sore throat and earache and were eventually cured by tonsillectomy at the age of seven.

My mother's standard restoratives for any illness or discomfort were tea and lemonade, though not together of course. Lemonade eased headaches, fever, indigestion and a host of other minor ailments. There were always stone jars of the magic liquid, as well as ginger beer, stored on the cold floor under the long pantry shelf. Regular cups of tea throughout the day *'bucked you up'* whatever your state.

One of her many favourite sayings was: *'Tea, best beverage in the world!'*

Hampshire May 1941

My Own Darling Elsie,

Received your letter today. Well, my pet, you are waiting to know what sort of a day I had yesterday. Well I will try to give you a pen picture of all I did and what went on.

I left camp on a bicycle at six o'clock. There was a gale blowing but little rain and after a ride of over eighteen miles I reached Southampton station at seven thirty-five. I then entrained on the seven fifty-three reaching Fratton station at nine o'clock…..and at nine fourteen I left Fratton, arriving at Brighton at ten forty.

Everyone was pleased to see me……Their first words in unison were, how is Elsie and the children, and you can bet I was not slow in telling them how well you all are and what a lovely time I had on leave…Well love, having enjoyed my repast and the pleasure of seeing Mum again I made tracks for Hove.

I called at Grace's first but finding her out I went on to the Hotel. Old Dick was very happy to see me, also the chef and old George. Mr Kling was all talk……I then saw Olive who told Mrs Rabbits, and she sent for me at once. I found her very poorly but overjoyed to see me. She thanked me for your letters

13

and mine and said she does not write any more as it is too much for her. She sends her love to you and hopes that we shall be united again soon and that I shall be back at the Hotel…

I then went to see Grace [a friend]. She was just her usual self and Ian looks fine and has grown a lot. She wanted me to stay to dinner but I could not do that as Mum had my dinner waiting for me at home. I gave Ian 2/6 and Grace sent lots of love to you and the Nibs. Well love, I then hurried home to dinner to find Bill [brother] waiting to see me. He looks well and both he and Carrie send their love to you all. It was late by the time I finished my dinner and all thoughts of going out to our home were out of the question. In any case it would only upset me for I can't bear it if you are not there darling.

I had only a couple of hours before catching my train back so I had a sleep for I was feeling very tired. I left David's birthday card at Mother's for her to post as I want to make sure he has it by Monday. After tea I caught the five seventeen and got into Camp at ten o'clock…..

I had a shock when I got back as a night exercise was due to start at ten thirty and I had to take part in it, so it was after two o'clock this morning when I turned in and gosh was I tired. Anyway, although it was only four hours sleep it rested my limbs and I feel fine today….

I found Mother much better than I expected although poor dear she has gone very deaf. Everyone thinks you are wonderful, and I could tell them that and also that I love you so much. Although I enjoyed my day yesterday I thought what a world of difference it would have made if you had been there my treasure, but soon I hope it will be so.

Your ever loving and devoted husband, Vin.

Thursday. [Sept.? 1941]

It was with great joy I received the parcel this morning. It certainly is a lovely parcel, and bless you, you did not forget a single thing, even to the salt. The pears were so ripe they had squashed a bit but were still eatable. The plums were lovely, darling. The bread, butter, cheese and tomatoes are going to make a nice meal for me, and believe me I shall not give the apples away for you know how I enjoy an apple. I presume the Welsh heather is the piece my Elvina sent for me.

I feel like you about the time hanging so and wish I could go to sleep for a month or more and wake up on the train going home to you…. I should love to have seen Dad in the Home Guard parade and it is with pleasure I hear how well he keeps now. All my love to you my sweetheart.

Your ever loving and devoted husband, Vin

Chapter Two
Life on the Garn

We rarely saw Mr and Mrs Williams Top House but when they appeared at their gate, tiny, frail and incredibly ancient, I was too timorous to go anywhere near them. One day they stood there, Mrs Williams in her long black dress and bonnet, offering us some cake in her quavery voice. David hesitated only a second before taking a piece but I was frozen to the spot at the sight of their wrinkled faces and gnarled hands. No amount of urging could make me approach any nearer, so my mother accepted the cake for me, apologising for my shyness. Eventually this gentle old couple just faded away, relinquishing all earthly ties. Top House was empty for some while after that.

The Snooks (next door) and their grown-up son Bill were all very rotund and they had a dog to match, a large old snuffling brown and white Spaniel called Caesar. I can remember her now, shouting, *'Caesaah! Caesaah! Yer, boy. Yer, boy!'* Mrs Snook spoke in a loud raucous voice as though she were addressing you from the top of the mountain, quite unlike my softly-spoken grandmother with her low melodious tones. A rather bossy woman was Mrs Snook who always spoke her mind, but tiny Nan could put her in her place when necessary. Whenever anyone overstepped the mark with Nan she would say, *'Go on you, about your business,'* in a tone which brooked no back answer, accompanied by a dismissive flick of her hand.

Mrs Snook never petted us the way most grown-ups did but we occasionally edged and wheedled our way into her house, bit by bit, or perhaps Bill invited us in now and again; he was quite affable after a pint or two at The Whistle. We loved to admire Mrs Snook's collection of Staffordshire china dogs which were displayed on the mantelpiece, and she might even offer us a biscuit from the biscuit barrel on the sideboard. After that we looked around the kitchen but there was nothing much to do except nod *'how-be-you'* to Mr Snook and Bill who always wore flat caps, and white mufflers round their necks, even in the house. Bill had very ruddy cheeks, no doubt induced by frequent visits to The Whistle Inn.

Mr and Mrs Williams Bottom House (no relation to Mr and Mrs Williams Top House) we knew as Aunty Hannah and Uncle Arthur and we loved them. Aunty Hannah had a voice like a cracked triangle - she spoke in a kind of double-voiced metallic discord. She had grey hair drawn back in a neat bun, rosy apple cheeks and twinkling eyes. She would greet us in her two voices, *'Well 'ello, my lovelies, and how be you today?'* Then she would smother us in her ample bosom. Her door was always open to us and there was usually a treat. *'Come and see what Aunty Hannah has got for you today.'* Uncle Arthur took great pride in his beautiful rose garden. He grew them in a variety of colours and they all had the most heavenly scent. On summer Sundays he would take us into his garden to choose a rose to wear to Chapel. We walked carefully around the rows of white, pink, red and yellow flowers - it was always a difficult choice, but once it was made he would snip off the bud with a short stem and present it to us with warm delight.

This safe, closely-knit world gradually expanded to include acquaintances further a field. David, who was mad about horses and longed to have one of his own, would sometimes wander off to visit Jessie Jenkins, a farmer who kept horses. One day Jessie said, *'Would you like to buy one with your pocket money, Dai-boy?'* and David immediately proffered a bag of three penny-bits he had apparently saved up with just such an offer in mind. Jessie chose a lovely brown pony, put a piece of string round its neck by way of a halter, and gave the end of the string to David. He proudly led the pony home, and into Grancher's workshop for a makeshift stable, and shut the door, believing he now really owned the horse.

Jessie, of course, had only been teasing, and when our Mother came home she had to explain to David that he couldn't keep the pony. David was heartbroken, but it was no use, horse and boy had to be separated. Mam was furious as she chased the little pony all the way back up the mountain. Jessie Jenkins was leaning over his gate, chewing a piece of straw and chuckling away at this unusual sight. But he got more than he bargained for. Mother not only returned the horse, she gave him the sharp end of her tongue, something to be reckoned with. He was never again known to *'sell'* horses to small boys as a joke.

Another man who kept horses was the father of my best friend, Pat Young. Her older brother Glyn was an Army Captain serving in India. She lived in the upper row of old houses. Mrs Young was kind-hearted but firm, well respected in the village, always ready to do a good turn for her neighbours, but strict in her observance of the Sabbath. One Sunday afternoon when I had been invited up there after Sunday School, she asked me what my mother was doing.

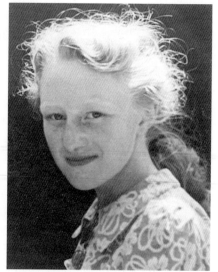

Pat Young, best friend.

16

I innocently replied that she was at home doing her knitting. *'Well just you go home and tell her to put it away,'* said Mrs Young, *'the good Lord made the Sabbath for a day of rest.'* Another time, at a Chapel function, she was sitting opposite a younger woman in a low-cut dress who leant across the table displaying an ample bosom. *'Eh, you d' want some salt and pepper on them,'* she said, and with that she picked up the cruet and liberally sprinkled the offending bosom. At this, the young woman roared with laughter, hugely enjoying the joke.

But she also had a reputation for acts of kindness. One day, Mr Young was coming up the track from the main road when he met a neighbour, a noted scoundrel, who looked astonishingly clean and smart, quite different from his usual scruffy appearance. When he got home he mentioned this to his wife. *'I've never seen Reggie look so smart.'*

'Well so he should - they're your clothes he's wearing!'

'What! You gave him my clothes! What did you do that for?'

'Well, he's going to Court and he hadn't any decent clothes to wear, so I gave him a shirt and a suit of yours"

'Well, I don't want them back!'

Mrs Young and Pat were very amused by her Dad's reaction.

The Youngs owned a field which sloped down steeply below the top row of houses and contained a stable with two horses. In the summer, Pat's father made a swing for us, a stout plank attached to two thick lengths of rope securely hung from the stable doorway. We spent hours playing on the swing, rolling in the meadow and telling each other all our secrets. In May and June the grass grew high and the field turned into a meadow full of wild flowers. Sometimes there were pony rides, and occasionally we would have the thrill of driving to Sunday School in the pony and trap. In late summer a tractor was brought in and we had fun helping to make bundles of hay for the horses' winter feed.

When the weather was wet, we played indoors with dolls and toys, and board games such as snakes and ladders, ludo, and Chinese Chequers which was my favourite because of the oriental decorations and brilliant jewel colours of the chequers. Then there might be an invitation to stay to tea, with the possibility of newly-laid brown boiled eggs. Whichever house we were in, the one who was visiting never wanted to go home, so one of us would whisper, *'I'll ask Mam if you can stay to tea.'* The invitation was usually given and accepted for the Youngs, like us, always had plenty of eggs from their hens, if not much else. Who could ever grow tired of those large brown eggs with their rich golden yolks so full of flavour?

'Houses' was a game we played outside, choosing a large open space on a fairly flat part of the rough mountain which was our natural playground. Sometimes it turned into 'mothers and fathers', but building the house was absorbing and could take all day so you might not get as far as mothers and fathers. One girl always had to take the role of father, of course, as boys were never allowed to join in. The house could have as many rooms as you wished, provided you could find enough small stones, as a single layer of these was used to map out the design of the house and represent the dividing walls of the rooms. Then we looked for pieces of pottery thrown onto the ash-mixen: broken cups and saucers, plates, jugs and bowls, often bone china in beautiful colours and patterns. We washed them in the brook, then we could really begin to live in our house, particularly if we had built it round a few large flat stones to serve as table and chairs. We also pretended to cook using leaves for cabbage and stones for potatoes, and sometimes we made 'ice-cream' with wet mud wedged between two 'wafer' slates.

One day after playing this game, Pat and I sat down together and wondered what it would be like to be really grown up and married. We decided we didn't like men very much; their faces and clothes were rough when they picked you up for a kiss, or caught you between their knees teasingly and refused to let you escape. Besides, you could never be sure of them. Sometimes they were gruff and bad-tempered, and at other times they were disconcertingly jolly, particularly when they smelt of beer or whiskey. At that time we came to the most serious decision of our young lives: when we grew up we would not marry men; if you had to get married, we would marry each other.

Glad and Tom Walby.

Aunty Glad was married to Uncle Tom, and for several years they lived with Nan but when the house next door to Pat Young became vacant, it was scrubbed out, newly painted, linoleum placed on the floors, curtains hung at the windows, basic furniture moved in, china hung on the pantry shelves, and as soon as the kitchen fire was lit it became home. Aunty Glad was once described by a

Uncle Tom and schoolboy Arthur.

family friend as the *'nearest thing to an angel on earth'*, the goodness fairly shone out of her. This is not to imply she was in the least bit weak and wishy-washy, she was quietly and strongly determined with a gentle but irrepressible sense of humour. My grandmother had nursed her through many a childhood illness, the most serious being rheumatic fever which had left her with a weak heart. Now she was married, the doctor warned her not to have any children as he feared the strain on her heart would be too great. Eleven years after this dire warning my cousin Janice was born. *'Well, you have your family now,'* said Dr Hind, *'but no more babies, mind, or I won't answer for the consequences.'* Two years later, Janice's sister, Pauline, entered the world. Now Tom and Glad had their family and they were content.

Uncle Tom worked down the mines. His hands were covered in scars from pick and shovel and scrabbling at the coal with his bare hands. The scars were deeply ingrained with black which no amount of scrubbing would ever remove. However, there were pithead baths where the miners could wash away the thick black grime which completely coated them and go home looking respectable. Occasionally, there was a breakdown at the baths, and then the men would have to go home to bathe. The first time Pauline, as a toddler, saw her father black from head to toe with only the whites of his eyes visible, she screamed the house down. This may have been an early indication of her vociferous nature; from a young age she was known to give her opinions firmly and sometimes sharply.

This spirited and lively appraisal of the world contrasted with her elder sister's laconic temperament, but later on, Janice's gently ironic remarks could be just as effective as Pauline's crisply delivered cuffs. Their looks were as widely contrasted as their temperaments: Janice was a dark-eyed beauty with jet-black

Pauline and Janice Walby.

hair, while Pauline had a snub nose, fair freckled skin, shrewd blue eyes and a shining head of rich auburn hair. Later on, when spending holidays in Hove, they were joined by my little sister who had rosy cheeks and a mop of golden curls. You can imagine people's amazement as Aunty Glad took this trio of little girls along the seafront: the blonde, the brunette and the redhead.

Let me return to the world of the Garn, however. Aunty Glad's house was as open to us as my grandmother's. I now spent every Saturday with her, and we were often all together in one house for meals on Sundays. Friends sometimes joined us for tea, the most frequent visitors being Aunty Glad's close friends, the Hills, who kept a sweet-shop in nearby Blaenavon. They had a grown-up son, Emlyn, who had a club foot and a withered left hand and arm. I was curious about Emlyn as he seemed different from other young men, although he was certainly not feeble-minded. I was intrigued by his dexterity in drying-up the dishes after a meal. He would fix a piece of crockery into his paralysed left hand whose wrist was permanently bent inwards, and proceed to dry it up using the teacloth in his good hand.

David and I were usually sent out to play after the meal. One day, as we ventured back in through the door we heard frightening noises and then witnessed a shocking scene. Emlyn was lying on his back on the floor, thrashing around with his arms and legs and foaming at the mouth while his father was kneeling over him trying to hold down his flailing limbs, and shouting at him, shouting his name over and over. Uncle Tom was trying to help Mr Hill but the others were just standing around watching. As soon as my mother caught sight of us she shooed us outside again. This scene terrified me but I could not bring myself to ask any questions, and I don't remember that any explanation was ever given to us. In time we learned that poor Emlyn suffered from grand mal epileptic fits.

Gladys and Marion on draw bridge over canal at Govilon, 1938.

Janice also told me that the Hills set up the sweet shop as a source of income for Emlyn, knowing he would never be able to take on a job. Apparently Mrs Hill started this quite simply by placing a box of chocolates in her window which fronted onto the street and gradually acquiring customers.

Now they were living on the upper row of houses, Glad and Tom were getting to know their neighbours and very soon discovered that, while some of them were lovely people, domestic harmony was not enjoyed by everyone. Sometimes the rows spilled out onto the bailey in front of the houses. On one such occasion a very large man, called Mr Beynon, had come home drunk and was ranting at his wife for supposedly carrying on with another man, and then Aunty Glad saw him punch her in the face. Imbued with her father's strong sense of justice, Gladys grabbed a broom and went out and whacked him with it. His wife showed her gratitude by not speaking to Aunty for several months.

However, this was a mild display of abuse compared with another neighbour who had a raging temper when he was drunk. Any money that came into the house was spent at the Whistle. The family might have starved if it hadn't been for the generosity of neighbours, and since there was no money for coal he started breaking up the furniture for firewood.

One night there were blood-curdling screams as one of the girls came racing along to Glad and Tom's and banged fiercely on their door. Her face was as red as a glowing fire and she continued to scream unmercifully. There had been an incident with a kettle of boiling water and her face was badly scalded. Fortunately, Uncle Tom was not on night shift and he had his special first-aid box at home with him. There were often accidents underground and he was used to dealing smartly with any emergency. Janice remembers him taking out some brown liquid and covering the poor girl's face with it completely. This prompt action healed her face, and she always marvelled that there was no scarring.

A couple of years later, when the Walbys were just arriving at Nan's house on a wild, stormy autumn night, they heard a man's cries for help coming from the direction of the brook. Tom forced his way through the wind and rain and with his torch made out the struggling bulk of someone in the swirling, swollen brook. He jumped into the turbulent waters and somehow managed to pull the drunken man to safety. Aunty Glad was terrified her husband was going to drown as well, and when the wife found out she said, *'Why didn't you just let the old bugger drown?'*

Chapter Three
Sunday School and the Welfare Hall

Every Welsh valley had its chapel and ours was no exception. *'Horeb Baptist'* was written over the door and religion played a large part in the life of the community. During those war years every pew was filled morning and evening, and the children filled the adjoining hall for afternoon Sunday School. One particular Sunday stands out in my memory. As the youngest group all sat round in a circle, the teacher asked me, *'Elvina, who is your neighbour?'* and I replied confidently, *'Mr and Mrs Williams, Top House; Mr and Mrs Williams, Bottom House; and the Snooks next door.'* I couldn't understand why all the other children laughed. Then the teacher recounted the Bible story of the Good Samaritan, and even I understood that my neighbour was anyone who needed my help. There was also an Anglican church in the village and I suppose it was regularly attended though I never remember knowing anybody who was church instead of chapel. *'Chapel, are they?'* was a legitimate first question to ask about any new acquaintances. This was the standard test to distinguish them from us.

People came to the chapel from miles around, most notably a large family of very beautiful children, always immaculate, who walked over from Waun Avon every Sunday. The eldest girl, Helga, was a best friend of my mother's. She came to Hove every summer to be fattened up as she was very slender. I believe they all had film star names such as Veronica, and Ingrid, who was nearest in age to me.

Horeb Chapel was situated in a hollow fifty yards below the unhappy Co-op and looking towards the mighty Coity. It was a plain and simple building with grey walls on the outside. Inside, the walls were painted duck-egg blue and hung with romantic pictures of Jesus surrounded by children of all nations and colours,

Helga Aylett.

or Jesus giving the people a nature talk about lilies, or Jesus helping a dazed Lazarus to rise from his bed. I loved looking at these pictures; the people in them had such happy, tranquil faces, and they kept me amused during many a long tedious sermon from the minister.

We attended at least twice on Sundays, morning chapel and Sunday School. The hymn singing was uplifting as the tunes were good and the congregation enjoyed making a joyful noise unto the Lord; singing in harmony was second nature to them with that special resonance and quality of voice which is native to the Welsh. Two of my favourites were *'Summer suns are glowing over land and sea/Happy light is flowing bountiful and free/ Everything rejoices in the mellow rays/All earth's thousand voices sing the psalm of praise'*, and *'Up from the grave he arose/With a mighty triumph o'er his foes/He arose the victor from the dark domain /and he lives forever with his saints to reign./He arose, he arose/Alleluia Christ arose'*, with the deep bases echoing *'he arose'* in the penultimate line.

The big event of the chapel year was the Sunday School Anniversary which took place in May. Every child was decked out in new clothes for this grand occasion. Just off Broad Street, Blaenavon, was Auntie Anna's children's clothing store where my brother and I were fitted with our anniversary outfits: smart shirt and trousers for David, a dress and bonnet for me. In 1943 my dress was in peach coloured silk with a scalloped hem edged with lace and delicate little flowers which were repeated around the neck and short sleeves. My bonnet was also bedecked with flowers and peach ribbons. The outfits were completed with new shoes, either black patent leather or white kid, and always knee-length white socks. It was necessary to save hard for money and clothing coupons to buy these outfits, as clothes as well as food were on ration.

For weeks before the big day we had to practise our recitations. On the afternoon of Anniversary Day all the children sat on the platform in tiered rows in their shining new clothes. Then as each name was called out, beginning with the youngest, they had to walk to the centre front of the platform and perform their recitation for the crowded congregation. It was quite an ordeal, and woe betide any child who let their family down by not standing up straight or speaking clearly.

Only a year ago my father had been with us on his final leave before going overseas.

…..Yes I remember only too well how I sat with you last year listening to all the dear children, and how well I enjoyed every minute of it. My heart was heavy at that time for I knew I was shortly to go away and its been a very long and lonely year. What I would not give just to have a peep at you all but my heart is with you always and I know that every day is a day nearer you….. when all this wicked war is over.

It's a year ago now since I was with you and it's been an age to me. I can see you now as I write this, standing by the wall below Mrs Williams' house bravely waving to me which was the start of my long journey away. I carry that picture of you standing there for I know next time we shall be running to meet each other….. We alone know sweetheart what this parting is and that constant longing to be together again. All love etc.

The following year my father sent a poem he had written for me to recite at the Anniversary.

Daddy

There's lots of us have Daddies
Who are so far away
And all of us are waiting
For that home-coming day.

But in this time of waiting
With thought sincere and true
We'll ask the good Lord Jesus
To see them safely through

Each night we'll say a little prayer
For those we love so dear
And if we are sincere enough
The Lord above will hear

So when I go to bed each night
Beside my bed I'll kneel
And ask the good Lord Jesus
To hear a child's appeal

God bless my soldier daddy
To war he had to go
Protect him from all danger
Because I love him so

Take care of him while fighting
Don't let me pray in vain
God bless my soldier daddy
And bring him safely home again.

Mother, Elvina and David.

Note: My father said in a letter that he remembered reciting the last few lines as a small boy when his own father was away fighting in WWI.

The war effort urged us all to make everyday objects at home out of scraps of this and that. Nothing was discarded and great ingenuity was employed in saving, making, mending so that waste was cut to a minimum. Cardboard milk bottle tops were washed and dried, then covered with coloured raffia and sewn together to make shopping bags and table mats. Any old clean clothes or rags were cut into strips and pushed through large oblong pieces of canvas with a large bodkin to make rag rugs. No fireside was complete without one, and they made a welcome addition to the bedroom, sparing the shock of feet meeting cold lino on first climbing out of bed, especially in winter. Old jumpers and cardigans were unravelled and the wool wound into balls to make new garments. As soon as girls learned to knit at the age of five or six they were set to work making dishcloths from a dreary greasy grey yarn on very thick needles. The dishcloths were then given to grown-up relations as Christmas presents!

Whatever we could do at home would help the war effort, and by extension our boys at the front. In addition, there were fund days when miniature Union Jacks were sold. I had no notion what the money was being collected for but it seemed to me a very good idea. So I coloured a page of my exercise book with little Union Jacks, cut them out, and went round selling them to the neighbours - until my mother found out! I couldn't understand why she was so cross as it seemed a good way of earning some money but I didn't make the mistake of doing it again.

Another war effort was the production of coal. The government balked at sending women down the mines so there were still men on the Garn. Their leisure time was spent in the Welfare Hall, enjoying a smoke and a game of billiards. There was a stage at one end of the large hall where my mother and her sisters had performed in choirs and operettas in their youth. The Welfare Hall ladies' committee suggested putting on a show with the proceeds of ticket sales going towards the war effort. The show would consist of a series of short items, mostly musical but with some short sketches.

Maisie Gwylym Davies outside Welfare Hall.

All little girls between the ages of four and six were invited to take part in the opening number, singing a lullaby to their dolls. 'Next week,' said the senior lady in charge, *'I want all you little girls to bring along your favourite doll to the rehearsal.'* Now she didn't say *'best'* or *' cleanest'*, she said favourite, so she was horrified when I turned up with Dinah. Dinah was really scruffy and her face was filthy, but she was my favourite doll because she was not made of cold hard china, but had a soft face which you could plaster with make-up and I had given her a specially large bright-red mouth for the show. The ladies were in flurries of consternation, they tut-tutted and conferred, and offered me a spare doll - hard china, clinically clean and totally lacking in character. I was adamant I would only take part if Dinah came too, so they reluctantly sighed and gave in.

My disgrace did not end with Dinah, however. On the night of the concert, when I looked out at the audience, there were Mam, Nan and Aunty Glad all vigorously waving, so I waved back, forgetting strict instructions to the contrary. Then during the lullaby I noticed some white specks on my black patent shoes so I bent down and polished them with my hanky, causing much amusement in the audience. The show ended with a rousing strain of *'Keep the home fires burning'* and then everyone stood to sing the National Anthem. When I first heard this most patriotic of songs in Wales, I thought, after the initial couple of lines, it went like this: *'Send him victorias, R.P. and glorias'* because of the wonderful Welsh accent. I knew *'victorias'* must refer to Aunty Solley's favourite plums, but I had no idea what R.P. and glorias meant. Similarly, at school, when we finished the day with communal singing, no words were handed out, and I was very puzzled by `*My body lies over the ocean'* and even more by `*Bring back my body to me'*. How could anyone do that?

The show had created work, excitement and a sense of achievement amongst those taking part, but once it was over life on the Garn quickly resumed its quiet pace, and evenings were spent playing games and listening to the wireless. Occasionally we went to the pictures in Blaenavon. Films were shown at Top Hall and Bottom Hall (indicating their positions in the main street). It was here I first made the acquaintance of stars like Charlie Chaplin, Stan Laurel and Oliver Hardy, Humphrey Bogart and Lauren Bacall, Merle Oberon and Douglas Fairbanks. When the film ended we poured out of the Hall into the pitch black streets with just a torch to light our way to the bus stop. The bus, when it came, had blinds drawn at all the windows for the blackout was imposed on buses too. The driver called out the familiar names of the bus stops: Cae White, Bunkers, Garn School, Lower Garn, and then the one we had been waiting for, the Garn. David and I were roused from our sleepy perch on someone's friendly bosom ready for the short walk up the mountain. Too tired even for hot milk, all we wanted was to get undressed and into bed with a comforting hot water bottle.

The winters were long and hard with tons of snow transforming the landscape into a picturesque wonderland. Between the snow in winter and the frequent rain during the rest of the year, Wellingtons were worn more than shoes. We could not afford luxuries like fur boots so we wore several pairs of socks inside our boots; even so, almost everyone suffered from chilblains, so great was the temptation to toast one's toes by the open fire. My cousin Margaret, a year of two older than I, once told me that if you buried your bare hands underneath the snow for five minutes you would never again suffer from cold hands. I tried this painful experiment once, and once only, and can assure you it does not work. In fact, it probably encourages the rheumatism so rife in the land of eternal rains (never mind the mist and the wild), and thereafter you feel the cold more keenly. The cold, however, did not prevent us from enjoying the snow. Well wrapped up with scarves and mittens, we played snowballs and built snowmen, but eventually, when the wet snow was down our necks and in our boots, and mittens were sodden, we returned home to thaw out in front of the kitchen range where all the clothes had to be dried.

Snowdrifts often prevented us from getting to school in winter, or the outside lavatories were frozen and we were sent home. The pond on the opposite side of the road from the school was a great attraction at dinner playtime when it was frozen hard and we could slide all over it. But then the big boys, not content with having fun, set about breaking up the ice and hurling huge chunks onto the steep banks. I once slipped on one of these and was slithering uncontrollably towards the icy pond when it seemed by some miracle I stopped at the edge. I can still recall that moment of intense fear for I would most likely have drowned in the icy waters.

There was another time when all three of us (Mam, Davy and I) might have drowned. It had been raining heavily for several days when Mam was getting us ready for school.

'Elsie, you are never taking those dear children to school in this atrocious weather.'

Mother.

'Yes I am, Mam, you know how important their education is to Vin and me.'
'But I've just yeard from Bill Snook that the brook is flooding over the bridge.'
'Well, I'll carry them across.'
'Do be careful, my girl.'
'Don't worry, Mam, I'll manage.'
'So long, Nan.'
'So long, my lovelies,' and she reluctantly waved us off into the storm.

We struggled down the lane, battling against the wind and rain and reached the overflowing brook. Its raging brown waters were swirling over the bridge which had no handrails. *'Right, then, David first,'* and she picked him up and slowly and carefully made her way across the treacherous footbridge, and placed him down safely on the other side just before a great surging wave rushed over. Then she made her way back for me. As she struggled across, desperate to keep her balance, I glanced down at the turbulent waters with fascination and terror. One slip, and we would have been swept down into the rushing stream and lost forever. But we safely arrived on the far side, and Mam heaved a huge sigh of relief as she set off again for the main road and the bus to school, her Nibs clinging tightly to her sides like two little monkeys.

After the long winter, signs of spring were a great thrill, and the many wild flowers that appeared in succession in the fields were greeted with wonder and excitement as we walked home from school. When you are only five or six you have experienced so few springs, and only three that you can remember, but the magical appearance of daisies and buttercups brings recollections of the previous spring, and a budding awareness of the unending cycle of nature. We sat in the fields and made daisy chains, then hunted for ladies smock, the exquisite pink flowers that grew by the brook. We pulled up rushes and sucked their succulent roots, then we pealed them and chewed the dry ridged inner stalk; we also picked the mauve flowers of thistles, prized for the nutty, milky interiors. Our landscape was devoid of hedges (gardens and fields were enclosed by dry stone walling) and boasted very few trees, but amongst the flowers and grasses we found a variety of things to chew, and the only wonder is that we didn't poison ourselves.

Apart from the dismal Co-op there was only one other shop on the Garn, Mr Painter's general store at the end of the Black Rank. The end houses were much bigger than the others, so Mr Painter had turned one of his front rooms into a dark little shop with a heavy oak L-shaped counter behind which the tinned and packaged goods were stacked on shelves. The vegetables were in big open sacks on the floor on the customer's side of the counter, but of course there was no such thing then as *'self-serve'* - the very idea would have been met with indignation and strong resistance. Customers only handled the goods after they had been paid for.

I was about five years old the first time I begged to be allowed to go shopping on my own. So my mother gave me a shopping bag and a purse containing a little money. A rehearsal was necessary first: Please Mr Painter, can I have a pound of potatoes?.......Please Mr Painter, can I have a pound of potatoes? Please Mr......That's right. Off you go then.

This was the most exciting adventure to date and I felt like a grown-up. All the way down the mountain I repeated the magic words over and over again, like a chant, getting faster and faster each time. I stepped into the shop with awe and was confronted by the imposing personage of Mr Painter himself. When serving, he always wore a dark grey overall and a brown Trilby hat, and looked at customers as though they were intruding and had no right to be in his shop at all. He regarded this mite of humanity over stern spectacles and then boomed, *'What can I do for you, Miss?'* My heart was beating so fast I almost turned and fled, but I managed to stand my ground, and in a tremulous voice blurted out, *'Please-Mr Potato-can-I-have-a-pound-of-painters?'*

Marion, Nan, Mam, Dad (Elvina in pram)
Coronation Day 1937.

Chapter Four
The Widening World

Avril was dainty and pretty with long golden brown hair and she was exactly my age. Also like me, she had a younger brother called David. My introduction to Avril and her family stands out in my memory for one reason: her father was rather small and I remarked with a five-year old's insensitivity, *'Aren't you little, Uncle John?'* and endured a severe telling-off from my mother. Avril's mother was still referred to by her maiden name of Doris Preece and came from a family of several sisters. At the age of eighteen, like other young girls from the Garn, including my own mother, she sought adventure in the southeast corner of England. There she met and married John Yeoman from Maidstone.

That summer the Yeomans had travelled to Wales in a little black car to visit Doris's family. (Inevitably, there were mutterings here and there of some people doing all right out of the war while others had to go and fight.) In spite of my faux pas, to my great delight, they invited me to go on one of their outings. It was not only the car ride I enjoyed but also the picnic tea Avril's mother provided: cakes and sandwiches were attractively set out on a gingham tablecloth. To me this was heaven, that you could have a meal out in the open air. After this experience I was mad about picnics and begged my mother every fine day to let me have a picnic. I did not care whether anybody joined me or not, I was quite happy to sit alone up on the mountain behind the house, enjoying my chocolate spread or marmite sandwiches. After all, everybody knows that food tastes much better in the open air, and best of all in the pure mountain air.

Sometimes at the weekend we went for long walks up over the incline on the opposite side of the valley from the Coity, passing by the balance pond and other signs of earlier mine workings. Then down into another valley, prettier than ours, where a canal was cut into the hillside, and we would stop for a rest in the attractive twin villages of Gilwern and Govilon, quenching our thirst with a drink of fresh milk from a farmhouse. Our goal was the small market town of Abergavenny, nestling at the foot of the Sugar Loaf mountain. This was also a favourite Sunday School outing when many families would join in and it took on the appearance of a pilgrimage.

On the seemingly barren slopes of the Coity mountain, apart from purple heather, there grew tough little shrubs which bore the most divine fruit in the world - whimberries. In late summer nearly everyone joined a whimberry-picking expedition, scrabbling up the sides of the mountain with their baskets in search of a glut of these small black berries with a flattened top, similar to a blueberry but, to my taste, infinitely superior in flavour. The children probably ate more than they contributed to the baskets, their lips and tongues bearing tell-tale dark purple stains. After a couple of hours of back-breaking work, the pickers descended with their baskets brimming with shining bounty, eager to make a whimberry tart for tea. The acknowledged champion of whimberry tart making was Aunty Glad whose meltingly sweet light pastry complemented this exotic fruit to perfection. Revived by memory, I can still taste it now.

Shopping expeditions there were in plenty and we had the choice of all the small towns there were round about. Blaenavon was the nearest and most familiar, but we also went to Brynmawr, Abergavenny, Ebbw Vale, and sometimes further afield to Pontypool and Newport. Blaenavon's shops were mainly in Broad Street and nearby. Here you found the grocers', greengrocers', clothes shops and shoe shops, and Jones Ironmonger who sold everything from washing soap, matches and candles to paint, pails and nails. If we were with Aunty Glad we always called into the sweet shop up the hill to see Mrs Hill and Emlyn.

Brynmawr was an extremely bleak and uninteresting place, but it had an open market on Fridays, and from there you could take a bus to Ebbw Vale - a place I hardly remember but the name always sounded romantic. Descending into Abergavenny on the bus was like entering a different world where everything was clean and green, devoid of slag heaps and mining machinery. This was treated more like an outing than a mere shopping expedition. The same with Pontypool because the park was a great attraction, with swings, a roundabout and a slide, and lawns sloping down on either side to the river running through. The park was surrounded by a wall with high wrought-iron gates at the entrance, locked at night, and stone steps leading down to the pathways. It was here I saw my first black soldier and could not help staring, so the image of him is etched in my memory. Usually the visit was rounded off with a visit to a teashop for tea and pastries which was a great treat.

Outings to Newport were rare and not exactly enjoyed as far as I was concerned, for the journey took an hour and a quarter and I was always sick on the bus. Once when the Solleys were staying we all went to Newport, including my grandparents and Aunty Glad and Uncle Tom, about ten of us altogether. Aunty Glad fainted while we were queuing for lunch at a restaurant. Everyone was concerned and Uncle Tom looked scared to death, but it was just the first intimation that my cousin Janice was on the way. On another occasion during Aunty Glad's pregnancy she was at the dentist's having a tooth extracted. Uncle Tom was in attendance and looked so terrified the dentist said, *'The trouble with some of you men is, you do love 'em too bloody much!'*

Restaurants during the war were able to provide only the plainest of fare and by the time we were served, the puddings had all gone. Great disappointment ensued. *'Well,'* said the waitress, *'we might be able to find some prunes and rice pudding for the children.'* *'Ugh, don't like prunes; ugh, don't like rice pudding,'* chorused David and I together. *'Shush,'* said the grown-ups, *'Be quiet!'* They graciously accepted the proffered pudding on our behalf for they, still hungry, were intending to eat it themselves.

Hereford, with its beautiful Cathedral and enchanting setting by the River Wye held the greatest charm. We wandered along the banks of the Wye looking for the most beautiful picnic spot. As we sat under the shade of a tree and gazed at the soft hills in the distance, my mother felt that the war must soon be over and peace restored to the nations. I'm sure it was her earnest prayer as she said to David and me, *'It will all be over soon and we shall be together with Daddy again.'* The courage of the men who went to war was matched only by the courage of the women who stayed at home.

While we were enjoying a warm, peaceful summer in Wales, my Father had embarked with thousands of other troops on a long sea voyage to the southern hemisphere, and around the coast of South Africa. He enjoyed at least one onshore leave before proceeding to his final destination - the North African Desert. Although he continued to write letters home, it was four months before he received any letters.

October 1942

......I am still without any news from England yet and up to now have not received any mail at all. I hope soon, however, to have all the back letters you must have written to me since I left. I cannot tell you just where I am out here but you will gather from the address I am with the Middle East Forces. It's all sand where we are and already I am longing for the sight of some green fields....

Then in April 1943 he received all his Christmas post.

I must tell you of the back mail I received today. It was all the Xmas cards sent to me last October so you see they've been six months reaching me..... I had a few sad minutes of deep thought and reflection when I received all those Xmas cards and a pang of homesickness engulfed me such as I had never had before…

I could not begin to tell you how very downhearted I am at times and what one has to endure out here but I know we are fighting a war, a war which means life or long lingering misery if we do not win. So I quit the grumbles and know only one thing and that's Victory. Every man Jack of us, no matter what part we play, has got to ensure that all freedom-loving peoples the world over have lasting peace and happiness…..

My love for you is as for my Country. You are my Country and the happiness I long for….so we must try not to get downhearted but think of that joyous reunion to come. Who can tell when it will be but it is the only thing I live and pray for…..

In November/December 1942 Dad went on a course and in the new year he was promoted to Sergeant. My mother sent him a telegram dated January 25th 1943 which read: Happy Anniversary fondest love and kisses congratulations on your promotion. He did not receive it until March, bearing nine post marks.

Later that year Mam had some surprising news to send to him. His cousin Frances who lived in Canada was now married to a Canadian solder, Walter Goodwin, and Walter's company had embarked for England. Imagine our surprise when Mam received a letter from him saying he was stationed near us, was due for some leave, and could he come and stay with us for a couple of days. So the visit was arranged and we looked forward to meeting our Canadian cousin by marriage. Looking back, my over-riding impression is of a very tall man who had to stoop all the time in Nan's kitchen to avoid hitting his head on the ceiling beams. But he also had a pleasant smiling face and a charming manner with a lovely Canadian accent. It was exciting for us to have a visitor who widened our horizons with tales of his homeland. It was a sad irony that Daddy, to whom he was most closely connected, would never have the chance to meet him.

Walter played games with us, took us out on trips and generally put all our lives on a higher plane for those few days. In particular, it must have given a much-needed lift to our mother who, I later learned, became quite depressed at times through missing Daddy and her home in Hove. No wonder she enjoyed her visits to London in spite of the dangers, and her regular trips to Brighton to see Nanny Hill, our paternal grandmother.

Chapter Five
The Garn School

Just over half way from Blaenavon to the Garn, just below the road, stood a yellow-brick building of unmistakable design: gabled with tall windows, an asphalt yard at the side, and protected from the road by a low wall topped with iron railings. This was Garn-yr-erw elementary School where my brother and I received our first years of formal education, as did our mother and her siblings before us. Indeed, one of her teachers, Mr Tully, was still there. Illness had prevented me from joining at the usual age of four but I started in the kindergarten

Garn School scholarship class 1928, Aunty Marion by Headmaster.

like everyone else. Here, the education was mainly centred around play, with building bricks and various other toys. There were paintings around the walls, original art by the youngest pupils, books on shelves and an abacus or two. We lined up in twos outside the classroom, one child being given a slate and the other a piece of chalk and we took it in turns to copy out letters written on the blackboard by the teacher, so along with play we gradually learned to read and write. Looking back, the process happened as if by magic for I cannot remember a time when I could not read.

At mid-morning recession we drank our free school milk and raced around in the yard. When a teacher blew the whistle we immediately stood stock still, then at the second whistle we ran to form lines outside the entrance, and when these were complete we filed into school, the youngest first. At dinner-time, hot meals were served in the hall at trestle tables covered with sickly-smelling oilcloth, usually cabbage, butter beans, a little meat and mashed potato - fresh fruit and vegetables were distinctly lacking. Attempting to swallow down these unappetising meals was a daily struggle. Once in the yard, however, the ordeal was quickly forgotten as we played with skipping ropes, whip and top, hopscotch or generally raced around chasing each other. There were also invented games, such as farmyard adventures with foxes killing chickens, and singing games such as The Farmer's in his Den and The Big Ship Sails on the Illey Alley Oh.

In the afternoon little camp beds were put up and we had to lie down for half an hour's rest. One particular afternoon, just as I lay down on my bed it collapsed at one end and my head hit the iron bar with a resounding thud as it struck the floor. Everyone thought this very funny except me, and I began to howl as I saw stars and felt the pain in my head.

Apart from that episode, kindergarten was a gentle introduction to school. However, we soon moved up to Standard One and the strict regime of Miss Prentice. She had very dark hair, dark eyes behind dark-rimmed glasses, a pale face accentuated by bright red lipstick, and a dumpy figure covered by a shabby flowery overall to protect her dress from the chalk dust. Occasionally she made us laugh with her dry sense of humour, but this in no way gave her the status of a normal person. Teachers, like doctors and ministers, were a race apart. Miss Prentice was

At Abersychan Grammar School, Aunty Marion back row right.

strict but fair, and for those eager to learn and willing to work, being in her class was no penance.

From the printing we had learned in kindergarten we now moved on to joined-up writing. Counting on the abacus prepared us for sums. Once we had mastered addition and subtraction we swiftly moved on to multiplication and division. Soon we were chanting our times tables every morning and by the age of seven we had learned our fourteen times table. Somewhere along the line we also made the progression from pencil to ink. The dry inkwells in our desks were filled every morning by the ink monitor, and each child was issued with a wooden pen holder sporting a shiny new nib. Many came to grief over this new obstacle in the path of learning. Blotted copybooks and ink-stained fingers causing nasty smudges dogged some pupils' efforts more than others.

Every day a short stocky fellow called John (nearly all the boys were called John) from a higher standard, who was unable to pronounce *'th'* came to check up on the attendance of the evacuees. Miss Prentice was never sure whether he was saying *'three'* evacuees or *'free'* evacuees (referring to those who were entitled to free school dinners). Of course, Miss Prentice's register was meticulous. Every morning we sat bolt upright in silence while she called our names in alphabetical order. We answered, *'Present, Miss'* and that was all. If anyone dared to utter another syllable we all had to sit with our hands on our heads. Then if the headmaster should chance to come in he would know someone had been talking, the greatest crime in school.

Megan Howells in Standard Four liked to rule the roost with a couple of cronies who were adept at twisting arms up behind backs and giving Chinese burns on the wrist. One day a tall new girl called Magda arrived and gave Megan a taste of her own medicine, soundly beating her in a fight. Megan, now a bedraggled and pitiful figure, began to cry buckets of tears. The humiliation of defeat was too much to bear. Suddenly, everyone's blood was up. Meg, after all, belonged to us and we closed ranks to protect our own. A council of war ensued. Sensing danger in the now hostile mood of the crowded playground, Magda darted up the steps, out of the school gate, crossed the road and headed for the tips beyond. The boys chased after her vowing to get revenge, while the girls comforted Megan. Much later the boys returned, looking sheepish rather than triumphant (so many boys onto one mere girl), and later still Magda limped into the yard, dishevelled, with a tear-stained face and nursing several cuts and bruises. Soon after that she left the school, but Magda had rendered us all a god turn as the episode changed Megan for the better.

I was also friendly at this time with Wendy Phillips, a bubbly girl with a sweet face which belied her somewhat mischievous nature. One of her favourite occupations was cadging food from friends and neighbours and especially from her own mother. One day Mrs Phillips made us bacon sandwiches, a rare treat. I can still remember the delicious taste of the crisply-fried home-cured bacon, with juices soaking into the fresh white bread.

Megan and Wendy introduced me to a new set of friends, older children who lived on farms at the foot of the Coity. On the farms we played wilder more exciting games, and used the farm outbuildings for hide and seek that could last practically all day on Saturday. As I was rather small, during one of these games Megan and Wendy had the bright idea of shutting me up in one of the small chicken coops. *'You'll never be found in there and you'll be the winner,'* they said. So I crawled into the chicken coop, half of which had a mesh-wire window and the other half a solid wooden door which they fastened. At first it was fun, this brilliant hiding place, but I seemed to be there for hours; the shouting voices died away, the light began to grow dim; I feared I had been forgotten. I began to shout. No one heard me. I shouted louder and louder, then began banging and kicking as much as my cramped quarters allowed. Eventually, one of the farm workers came by and let me out, chuckling to himself at the strange *'chicken'* he had found.

On warm spring and summer days our colt-like energy champed against the narrow confines of the playground. We divided haphazardly into teams of wild ponies and chased each other up and down and round about the small tips. We needed this release of energy before we could once more sit quietly at our desks and, like so many small genies in bottles, perform the wishes and commands of those controlling wizards, the teachers. Whether it was reading aloud, singing, mental arithmetic or, most terrifying of all, pandering to the whims of the Headmaster when he occasionally without warning came in to measure our progress, or perhaps to release Miss Prentice for an urgent visit to the dentist, we were urged to do our best.

Mr Jones's presence always struck terror into our young hearts. He always entered the classroom with lips parted in a smile that wasn't a smile, more a sarcastic leer. Wisps of white foam were permanently stuck in the corners of his mouth. He also had an unnerving habit of continually whacking his cane against his trouser leg (never without his cane, it seemed glued to his hand), a constant reminder we were utterly in his power. Had it not been for these unpleasant traits we would no doubt have enjoyed the occasional times he took over as he was full of ideas and loved mental puzzles and riddles. One of his favourites went like this: If there were twenty-six sheep in a field and one died how many were left? Put your hands up, don't call out! You, boy! His stick pointed at someone. Twenty-five, sir! Wrong! he replied with glee. All the hands went down. He repeated the puzzle once more, slowly. Puzzled frowns on every face. Mr Jones rubbed his hands with pleasure. Again the riddle, very slowly this time....Then two hands shot up. Yes, you at the back! Nineteen, Sir. Correct - you have the correct answer. Still many puzzled faces. He wrote the riddle on the blackboard: If there were twenty *sick* sheep in a field and one died ... A muffled groan went round the form at this sense of trickery.

When it was going-home time he rarely let us out all together. Rather, he would play some further game of suspense like starting with the end of the alphabet and announcing each letter slowly with long pauses in between. You stood up if your name began with that letter, and then when five or six were standing he would let them go.

What did we do when it rained, or indeed snowed in that mountainous region? There was a cupboard full of books, board games and jigsaw puzzles for those disposed towards quiet recreation. Surprisingly, those who wanted to make a noise and let off steam were allowed to do so (providing they didn't actually cause a riot). The older girls sometimes took over a spare classroom and aped the Hollywood dance routines, the high-kicking chorus lines they had seen in films. The younger girls begged to be allowed to join in, and soon almost every girl in the school was taking part in an impromptu show. When left alone we could enjoy ourselves in a highly organised fashion.

There was one disturbingly unpleasant episode that was not directly to do with school but something that happened on the way home. This particular day, all my usual friends had gone ahead, and there was just Jean Wilkins, a new girl, lingering at the gate, so I started walking along the side of the road with her (there was no pedestrian footpath). Suddenly, she looked round and said, *'There's a car coming - quick let's cross the road!'* I looked, saw the car, and hesitated. Jean darted into the road. What happened next I couldn't say for certain. Whether she fell over as the car screeched to a halt, or whether it actually knocked her down, I shall never know. She was badly shaken but only slightly hurt. The motorist was white as a sheet and desperately concerned.

That night, long after I had been tucked up in bed, I heard the arrival of a visitor and knew instinctively it was concerned with Jean's road accident. My mother crept upstairs and whispered to me to avoid waking David, *'Vina, there's a gentleman downstairs who wants to ask you a few questions.'* In great trepidation I entered the warm kitchen in my long flannel nightgown. The *'gentleman'*, a plain-clothes policeman, had removed his trilby hat but still wore his long mackintosh.

'Hello,' he said in falsely genial manner. *'Now I want you to think carefully and tell me exactly what happened when you and your friend were coming home from school today.'* I gave my view of the events. *'Are you sure Jean fell over, or did the car knock her down?'* I was not sure, but I thought she fell over - it all happened so quickly. He repeated his question over and over in many different ways - his few questions turned into a full-scale interrogation. He tried to put words in my mouth to force me to say it was the motorist's fault. It seemed Jean was adamant the car had knocked her down and my corroboration was required. This odious detective made me feel guilty, made me feel, in a sense, the whole episode would be my fault if I didn't give in and

agree with his prejudiced opinion. In the end, I believe I did, and it left me worrying for days that I had betrayed that poor motorist.

Private cars were few and far between in those days, and tanks and other army vehicles seldom passed through the Garn, so it was with great excitement that the word went round that an American jeep had parked outside the school and two American soldiers were talking with the Headmaster. Then all the evacuees were summoned to the hall where the American soldiers handed us large bags of candy, chewing gum, and huge novel activity books with pages for colouring and painting, and others with cut-out models of tanks, ships, planes and men and women soldiers. We felt very special to receive such generous presents from the Americans, and it certainly favourably coloured my view of the American nation.

Sweets were in limited supply, on ration, and sometimes there were simply none at all, so we found substitutes. Spanish wood, rather like a stick or twig, which could be sucked or chewed, was greatly enjoyed by some though I never acquired a taste for its strong flavour. Sometimes we managed to get hold of half a cut lemon which was dipped into a little bag of sugar- a substitute for sherbert. Chewing-gum, naturally, was highly prized for its status symbol, it made you feel grown-up and worldly, like an American. Its other advantage was that it could be made to last a long time. My mother, however, was terrified of chewing gum. *'You mustn't swallow it,'* she said, *'or it will stick to your heart'*! This dire warning notwithstanding, we took it to school in our pockets, along with any other treats we could smuggle out of the house, to be indulged in at playtime when a good deal of bartering took place.

David and I were thus formed and shaped by the formal and informal influences around us, the sound if rather didactic education, and the customs, habits, games and pastimes of our school friends. We had two long absences from the Garn School which we spent in London, the centre of the blitz, an enormous contrast to the peace and quiet of the Welsh mountains. How those visits came about is the subject of later chapters.

Chapter Six
Sweet as a Nut

War-time weddings were quite common especially amongst servicemen and women due to go overseas. Uncle Arthur was only twenty and already in the Royal Navy when he married his sweetheart, Mary Dando, in 1941 at Llanwenarth Baptist Chapel. They made a handsome couple, Arthur in his naval officer's uniform and Mary in a smart new suit and hat with a feather. Theirs was a simple affair with few guests in attendance. Time was of the essence as Arthur had only a few days leave.

Aunty Marion's wedding was altogether different. She married Uncle Ron at St. Peter's Church, Blaenavon, in September 1943, attended by three bridesmaids: Aunty Mary's sister Beryl, my cousin Margaret and Barbara Solley, with David as a pageboy and Elvina as a flower girl. I doubt that David was delighted at the age of five to be wearing long blue velvet trousers and a frilled white satin blouse and told he was a page boy, but all girls long to be a bridesmaid and I was no exception. My dress had a white satin bodice, layers of white net for the skirt, and was trimmed with blue velvet ribbon. We wore extraordinary headgear consisting of several layers of satin and net in ruched rounds, also trimmed with velvet, which were held onto the head with elastic. In the photographs they look rather like floppy layered pancakes. My hair was in fashionable ringlets achieved by torture. All night I had to lie in bed with my hair divided into sections, each section wound tightly around with long strips of rag. It was excruciatingly uncomfortable. But there, women have always been prepared to suffer for their beauty!

A studio portrait of Nan and Granch with the bridal couple reveals them to be well advanced in years. The circumstances of their hard lives made this inevitable. Nan was born Mary Ann Waters in 1882, the granddaughter of Irish immigrants. She grew up at Forge Row cottages, next door to the future Mrs Arthur Jenkins. The family was so poor that Mary Ann had to leave school when only eleven

Nan and Granch, wedding day, 23rd May, 1908 at Horeb Baptist Chapel.

Maternal great-grandmother, Elizabeth Whitney, with her first grandchild, Dorothea Davies.

and help her mother who took in washing to boost the family income. After a couple of years she went into service in a large house in Abergavenny where the people were very good to her. She became a lady's maid and learnt the ways of a lady which she considered the finest training she could have had. For many years after her marriage she continued to pay visits to her *'lady'* taking each of her daughters in turn. Girls in service were not usually allowed *'followers'* or *'gentlemen callers'*, and as they hardly ever enjoyed time off it's a wonder that any of them managed to meet any eligible young men.

However, Mary Ann did meet a young man named Thomas James Davies who used to trek over the mountains every evening after his shift in the mines to attend night school in Abergavenny, the place where Nan was working in a large house as lady's maid. As Tom had a sister also called Mary Ann he nicknamed his sweetheart *'Sal'*, a name which stuck for the rest of her life. He had been a keen scholar but had to start work in the mines at twelve years of age. Two of his sisters became school teachers and my mother has told me many a tale of Aunty Flora who eventually became a headmistress and was very strict.

Thomas managed to improve his learning and gained a fair education but he put it to the use of others rather than himself. He worked tirelessly for the miners, pressing for improvements such as pithead baths. He was always ready to help with writing letters and administrative matters. He also gave some assistance in the constituency office of Arthur Jenkins, M.P. , Roy Jenkins's father, and came to have such a

Marion and Ron, married 1943, St Peter's Church, Blaenavon.

Elvina and David.

standing in the community that he was made Chairman of the school governors. He was also Chairman of the Soup Kitchen Committee during the 1926 Miners' Strike and for this service he was presented with a gold watch and chain which is now in the possession of his son.

Work required one set of clothes, gardening another, but when my grandfather went about on business matters, a more smartly dressed gentleman you could not have wished to see. On these occasions he always wore dark three-piece pin-striped suits with his gold watch and chain hanging from his waistcoat pocket, shirts with starched collars, a smart tweed cap, highly polished black shoes and, if necessary, a long black overcoat. In his later years, although he was still upright and walked smartly, he carried a walking-stick.

Throughout his life he hardly knew the meaning of the word leisure. Occasionally, he had time to sit by the fireside in his special armchair reading the Daily Herald or perhaps to indulge in a drink with a friend or two at the Whistle Inn, or sit with a grandchild on his knee. But mainly his life consisted of work from the time he got up until he went to bed at night. His hobby, but also his means of supporting his family (and many others) in times of grave necessity such as the 1926 miners' strike, was gardening. He loved his gardens, especially his top garden with its adjoining field, where he could pause in solitude and survey the peaceful scene around him and feel the fresh mountain breezes blowing over him. An articulate man of sound moral judgement who fought against poverty, injustice and corruption wherever he found them; who spoke at meetings on the serious issues of the day; whose life was hard but found its greatest happiness in the home and family, he was ultra sensitive to personal criticism, but his soul found healing balm in the peace and quiet of his gardens while he turned over the rich black soil with an expertise born of long practice.

His wife was a small but dignified lady, with a low soft musical voice, very capable in running her home, serving on ladies' committees and helping in the community. Tom helped his wife to improve her reading and writing abilities and it was her pleasure to sit on the leather sofa of an evening underneath the window, her spectacles perched on her nose, reading the daily paper. Every so often she would draw in her breath and let out a sigh with an *'aye'* sound when something particularly affected her. She also enjoyed listening to the wireless.

Her life, too, had been relentlessly hard in its daily manual grind, but she worked her way methodically through the week, assigning various tasks to hours in the day and days in the week, not only washing and ironing, but jobs like black-leading the grate, scrubbing out the lavatory, and fetching washing water from the brook, and drinking water from the spout. The spout was a pipe coming directly out of the side of the hill about one hundred and fifty yards up the path beside the brook. Even when water was eventually supplied directly to the cottages from Grwyny Fechan reservoir, the spout continued to trickle forth its ice-cold liquid which we found very refreshing when we were playing near the old tips or in Grancher's top field.

If I came downstairs early enough in the morning I might catch Nan in her dressing-gown, her long grey hair (usually drawn back into a neat bun) flowing down her back, stamping on the *'black pats'* as she called the cockroaches which were never seen at other times of the day. Such things did not bother her: she dealt with them, and there was an end of it. *'Father'* did enough worrying for both of them, so *'Mother'* got on with life and its demands in her quiet way. She was most delightful when, as often happened, something tickled her sense of humour, and she either dissolved into fits of giggles, with her hands or apron hiding her face, or made soft infectious *'ho, ho, ho'* noises with her shoulders shaking and often tears streaming down her face. Then Granch would say, *'Well, well, what's tickled Mother's fancy now, I wonder?'*

Sometimes the cause was obvious, like the day she met the Londoner, Mr Basin. *'Excuse me, what did you say your name was?'* she inquired. *'Bison, ma'am, Bison - as in puddin' bison'* His broad Cockney accent, combined with graphic illustration was too much for Nan, she was just hysterical with laughter. Fortunately, Mr Basin took no offence. Another oft-told story was of a time when Aunty Solley was staying, sitting at the table and talking away with great animation as usual. She picked up the sauce bottle and shook it with enthusiasm, not noticing it was minus its top. As she talked and shook the sauce was going everywhere and Nan, seeing the funny side as usual, was too helpless with giggles to stop her. Eventually, Aunty Solley noticed the strangely splodged scene around her and realised Nan was not merely laughing at stories of London life.

Strangely, she was not always tolerant of giggling in others, and David and I were often admonished with, *'Now, now, stop it now! Laughing always comes to crying!'* If we did anything which displeased her or set her teeth on edge, she would complain with, *'Ach y fi!'* or *'Drabbity drow!'* Sometimes we naughty children then increased rather than decreased the offensive action, in order to tease her, but only if we knew she was in a good mood to start with. Nan was so good to us we didn't care to make her really angry. There was sometimes a treat which you weren't expecting, like a juicy pear taken from the linen chest where she had carefully stowed it away to ripen, or a piece of whimberry tart with some cold custard.

Nan was highly respected in the community, and a place or a seat at any gathering could always be found for her however late she arrived. *'Make room for Mrs Davies by there, will you?.......Yers a place by yer for Mrs Davies, look … Come and have this seat, Mrs Davies,'* and she would be comfortably settled down. She tried to protect Granch from the many folk who made demands on his time, requiring help with applications or form-filling, advice of one kind or another - or spare produce from his garden. Often a child came with the latter request and would go away with a full bag saying, *'Mam will pay you back.'* But *'Mam'* could rarely afford to pay back.

Nan and Granch with Elvina and David, 1938.

My grandfather became Check Weighman at the pit, the man the miners trusted to check the weight of the coal they produced and guard them from any sharp practices by the mine owners. He was known to the men as Tom Check but Nan, who rarely put on any airs or graces, thoroughly disapproved of this name. When any Tom, Dick or Harry came to the door enquiring for Tom Check, she would pull them up firmly with, *'There's no one yer of that name but if you do mean Mr Davies, then yes, he's at home.'* Granch could not bear anything mean or underhand. He put up with a lot from his employers and the government who were hand in glove with them, and suffered in silence. However, the one thing that embittered him was during the 1926 depression. The miners were out on strike, there was no money coming in and families were destitute. Those who had been thrifty and saved were penalised: all their savings had to be used, and even the small amounts of insurance they had paid in for their children had to be drawn out before any help was forth-coming. His utter disgust that they could rob the very children of the miners did not abate

Nan, aged 75.

when the strike ended. The memory was too bitter, and he vowed never again to save a penny in his life.

Granch, then, was a kind but rather serious man, with rare moments of fun, but often inclined to grumpiness, no doubt caused by the stomach and chest complaints from which he suffered. He was often ill with bronchitis. In his last couple of years he renounced his teetotal vow and took whisky to ease his stomach pains, but of course it made things worse, and he died in 1953 at the age of 73. There were obituaries of him in the local papers detailing his career of 58 years at the Blaenavon collieries. He was a vice-president of Blaenavon Colliery Band and held the rare distinction of being elected a life member of Blaenavon miners' lodge.

Nan never complained that I remember. If you found her rubbing her leg (probably to ease the pain of rheumatism) and asked, *'What's the matter, Nan?'* she would invariably reply, *'Nothing, my lovely, just a bit of old bone in Nan's leg, that's all.'* With such comments she would make light of any ailments. She slipped on ice one winter and broke her knee-cap at the age of sixty-seven and was told she might never walk again. But the doctors reckoned without the determination of Mary Ann Davies. She did walk again, and with almost her former sprightliness. Aunty Glad was the only other member of the family who remained living on the Garn so it fell to her to take care of Nan when she became forgetful in her later years. Every day she insisted they go up the mountain to the old house to light the fire *'to keep the place aired for when I return'* which of course was never going to happen. If anyone remarked to Nan, *'Gladys is very good to you, Mrs Davies,'* she would reply, *'They are all good to me, all my children.'*

'As sweet as a nut.' That's what the doctor said when she died in her sleep at the age of 79. There was no disease, no illness; her poor old tired body was simply too worn out to carry on.

Granch.

Chapter Seven
London 1942

Young children have an amazing capacity to adapt to whatever life brings. From the peace and quiet of the Welsh mountains, the slow pace of rural life, we were thrust into the crowded streets of London with its row upon row of houses, double-decker buses, the Underground and escalators, large buildings, exciting shops - and air raids. There was wonder, excitement, new and stimulating experiences, but we seemed to take it all in our stride. In spite of dangers, the metropolis offered new treats and opportunities which we embraced with delight.

Marie Solley was an extraordinary and charismatic personality. In any company her wonderful presence overflowed with generosity, good humour and sheer indulgence in the enjoyment of life, somehow contriving to overcome the privations of war, and carry along on the crest of her wave all who were responsive to her demanding but affectionate nature. From our earliest memories she was called Aunty Solley by David and me, and by this name she became affectionately known to the rest of our close family, though in his letters my father always respectfully referred to her as *'Mrs Solley'*. She was remarkably capable and could take charge of any situation, especially in the case of illness, birth or death which were much more neighbourly affairs in those days. It was my parents' good fortune to have such a neighbour in Hove when both their babies went down with a severe attack of whooping cough, and my mother soon afterwards had shingles. Nursed back to health, her babies taken care of, my mother felt the debt could hardly be repaid. Such a bond united our families that no amount of wars or removals could break the tie.

Barbara Solley.

The Hills evacuated to Wales, the Solleys removed to London, but occasionally the steam train from Paddington carried them on the Great Western railway line to Newport, and the hourly Ralph's bus brought them up the valley to Garn-yr-erw. Great were the rejoicings at these reunions although the rollicking fun and laughter sometimes proved overpowering for my quieter grandparents. I seem to recall that Uncle Charles, frail in health, usually stayed in

Charles and Marie Solley with David.

London. He was twenty years the senior of his wife, his temperament more sober and reflective. An artist by profession, he had formerly taught drawing at a boys' preparatory school in Hove, but he was now retired as a semi-invalid and occupied his time in making toys and gifts for friends. Their son, Charlie, was a charming and handsome teenager with plenty of girlfriends and his vivacious sister Barbara was still at school. Within a couple of years, Charlie had enrolled in the Merchant Navy and Barbara was training to be a nurse.

In the autumn of 1942 Aunty Solley became seriously ill, and with Uncle Charlie still unwell, Mam lost no time in packing a suitcase and whipping us up to London so she could nurse both Mr and Mrs Solley and take care of the household. As it was likely to be a very long visit we were both enrolled in the local infant school. My brother David, although only four at the time, said he can still remember the route we took to school every day.

The family now lived in a rather grand-looking house in Westcroft Square, Hammersmith. There was a large first-floor drawing room with a highly polished floor, a long table in the middle, and a leopard-skin rug with the leopard's head still attached. Our favourite game was to give each other rides round the room on the rug, seeing just how fast we could race around while the rider clung onto the leopard's head and tried to avoid banging into table legs or any other hard furniture, while getting dizzy in the process, and trying to avoid being flung off altogether. It was strictly forbidden and we got into serious trouble if we were caught but that made it all the more exciting.

I also enjoyed playing dressing-up games with my new-found London friends. Sometimes we paraded around the square in our mothers' dresses, long beads and high-heeled shoes - my favourite being a pink satin Charleston dress with a six inch sequinned fringe at the hem. We also coveted discarded handbags and scent bottles. Two of the most evocative perfumes I remember were Californian Poppy and Evening in Paris - a dark midnight blue bottle with silver printing. If the handbags still contained a few pennies, there was a little shop nearby where you could buy ice-cubes flavoured with orange - a pale forerunner of today's sophisticated ice-lollies.

School itself seemed much more free and easy and less formal than in Wales, perhaps because of the frequent interruptions caused by the bombing. Sometimes the teacher even asked us what we would like to do! This was not like school at all as there seemed to be hardly any work. I volunteered to recite a poem Aunt Marion had taught me, and the teacher was so delighted she sent me to repeat my performance to the class next door which happened to be where my little brother was, in the kindergarten.

Aunt Marion, my mother's younger sister, became a frequent visitor for she was a nurse at Hammersmith Hospital, taking care of wounded soldiers. She had been educated at Abersychan Grammar School, the same school that Roy Jenkins attended, in fact he was a contemporary there of Uncle Arthur's. Uncle said he was a political animal even then, arguing with fellow pupils on the long walk up the hill from the railway station. As Marion was my godmother she took a particular interest in my academic progress. She it was who first instilled in me a love of poetry and learning by heart. On one of her visits to Westcroft Square she met Aunty Solley's nephew, Ronald Horner, who was in the Royal Navy and they fell in love and soon announced their engagement, so now we had a real family connection.

One night when Ron was home on a forty-eight hour leave, he and Marion went to the pictures at a nearby cinema. During the film the screen suddenly went blank and a message was flashed up - *'Would Marion Davies and Ron Horner please go to the foyer at once.'* Shocked and embarrassed, they stood up and squeezed their way along the row of knees and feet until they reached the aisle where an usherette with a torch led them to the foyer. There was Aunty Solley waiting for them and her first words were, *'There is nothing to worry about.'* But of course that only half allayed their fears; they were anxious to hear the reason for this interruption.

It turned out that Arthur, Marion's younger brother and the baby of the family, now serving in the Royal Navy, had suddenly arrived on the doorstep of No. 27 (very few people had telephones in those days). He had been granted a twenty-four leave as his ship had docked in London and he was desperate to spend some of those few precious hours with his sister, especially as he knew no one else in London. Now this was just the sort of situation where Marie Solley could take charge. She left Arthur in the care of Babs and marched down to the cinema to speak to the manager. He was adamant he could do nothing to help as he did not regard this as an emergency, but the persuasive powers of our Marie were such that he relented when she pointed out that Arthur was on active service and might never see his sister again. So the reunion was effected.

Mary also came to stay that autumn. Aunty Solley invited her to Hammersmith when she was run down after nursing baby Julie for six weeks through a bout of whooping cough. I believe Arthur also managed a forty-eight hour leave at that time. What with Mary and Arthur, Marion and Ron, Babs, and young Charlie and his girlfriends, the house in Westcroft Square became uncomfortably full of cavorting couples in their teens and early twenties. Their horseplay sometimes got out of hand while David and I looked on with a mixture of fear and fascination. To our consternation, they played far more dangerous games than we did. My greatest fright occurred when they lifted up the sash window of the first-floor drawing-room, caught hold of Mary and pushed her half out of the window and held her there dangling backwards over the window sill while she screamed blue murder.

Mary and Arthur, married 1941, Llanwenarth Baptist Chapel.

How my mother coped with tending sick patients and looking after two young children while surrounded by a riotous rabble of courting couples I shall never know. But probably they all needed these high jinks to let off steam as a relief from the seriousness of the war. Mary has since told me how Charlie broadened her education during this visit by taking her to a night club and introducing her to the delights of caviar and champagne. Charlie was a waiter at a high-class gentlemen's club for the rich and famous. He had many fascinating stories to tell as well as occasionally being able to add luxury items to the household wartime fare.

Aunty Solley's health improved but the air raids became more frequent and night after night the siren went. David and I were taken from bed, wrapped in blankets and carried down the stairs and the outside steps, and across to the green square where two air raid shelters had been excavated. (On a recent visit to Westcroft Square I discovered that the mounds forming the roofs of the shelters can still be seen though they are disguised with a covering of turf.) All the Square's inhabitants were rushing across to one or other of the two shelters. Down the steps we went to our concrete tomb and sat on benches around the walls, all huddled up with our neighbours. Sometimes the *'All Clear'* would sound quite quickly, at others it would take hours. David and I loved these adventures in the middle of the night for Aunty Solley always gave us lemonade and biscuits when we were safely back in bed.

As Aunty was making such progress healthwise, we were able to go out much more to the West End and South Kensington to look at the large stores. Sometimes we went by bus but mostly we used the Underground which came out at the surface at Hammersmith and ran along the back of the houses in Westcroft Square. We could easily pick out No. 27 because of the yellow canary hanging in the kitchen window, and Aunty always said, *'Wave to Chippy in the window,'* as we went by.

David was undoubtedly Aunty Solley's favourite, the one she cuddled more frequently on her lap, but she delighted in spoiling us both and that season was fast approaching when spoiling is at its height. Christmas preparations were in progress, visits to Harrods, Selfridges and Gamleys became more frequent and the storage of extra food and luxury items, especially those meant to be a surprise on the big day, raised a few problems. More and more presents were stored at one end of the large drawing room and covered over with spare sheets. Of course this did not stop David and me peeping under the covers but our presents had been craftily hidden at the back.

On Christmas Day 1942, twelve people sat around the magnificent long dining table to enjoy the wonderful feast prepared by Aunty Solley and Mam. In the afternoon, as usual, Father Christmas arrived to distribute the mountain of presents. David and I had our wishes granted: my brother became the proud owner of a shiny scooter and I of a dolls' pram. No doubt they were second-hand items repainted, but none-the-less wonderful for that. I couldn't wait to parade my pram around the square, stuffed with my family of dolls and the envy of all the other little girls; and David needed no instruction in riding a scooter - he was soon whizzing round at top speed. However, there was one mishap which I vividly remember.

Father Christmas had been exceptionally bountiful that year, and along with the doll's pram, I had received a beautiful china doll. Now, I was not over-fond of china dolls as they were rather hard when you cuddled them, but one day when my friends were playing outside with their new dolls, I begged my mother to let me take Betty (as she had now been christened) to join them. *'No indeed,'* she said emphatically, *'you'll only go and break it.'* *'Please, please, please,'* I wheedled and in the end I got my way. While sitting on the stone front steps, the inevitable happened. The precious doll somehow slipped from my grasp and cracked her head on the stone staircase. Of course, I was mortified and my mother was very angry with me, but after receiving due punishment dear Aunty Solley assured me that as soon as the shops were open again Betty would be taken to the dolls' hospital to have her poor head bandaged and mended.

The highlight of the Christmas season that year was a visit to a West End pantomime, Cinderella. It was my first pantomime and made a great impression on me with all the different characters, colourful costumes, spectacular scenery, and of course the usual banter between characters and audience. My favourite scenes were those conveying the age-old story of poor Cinders, her maltreatment at the hands of her ugly sisters, and finally winning her Prince Charming. When the Fairy-Godmother waved her wand over the giant pumpkin and four white mice, they were miraculously transformed into a fairy-tale coach drawn by four real white ponies, their plumed heads nodding as they proceeded across the stage to the rapturous applause of the audience. It was a truly magical performance.

There were visits to the cinema some evenings and often to rather adult films, which either scared or bored us. But I vividly remember the Pathe News announced by the crowing cockerel showing film of the progress of the war and can still hear in my head the voice of the presenter. I also well remember the night a late-comer pushed his way along the row and then proceeded to sit on top of me - as I was so small he couldn't see me as his eyes had not adjusted to the dark - but my squeals of fright soon let him know I was not an empty seat. The cinemas were well patronised and often quite full for there was no television, and films provided entertainment and a means of escape for a few hours from the constant worry of the war. There were thousands of women like my mother who were anxious about their husbands, sons or brothers, who prayed nightly for their safe return but had no idea what was happening to them or even where they were stationed. They were not allowed to mention which country or even talk about their daily routine. My father often said these restrictions made it difficult for him to make his letters interesting, but he never failed to reassure my mother of his never-ending love for her and the children, or *'Nibs'* as he always called us.

Chapter Eight
Nanny Hill

There was another important guest of the Solleys that Christmas, Nanny Hill, my paternal grandmother, who lived in Brighton. During our time in Wales my mother sometimes returned to Brighton to visit her, and before my father was sent overseas they managed to spend a couple of forty-eight hour leaves together at her home. In a poignant letter to her son Vincent she tells him of the wonderful invitation from Mrs Solley and how she is looking forward to seeing Elsie and the children, and how she will enjoy having a rest. Those last few words say much about her life.

I have a dim memory of a frail-looking, gentle, white-haired old lady with a sweet but sad face. Widowed young, she must have had a difficult time bringing up her three boys, William, Vincent and Augustus (Bill, Vin and Gus) and a girl, Mabel (Mabs), on a very low income. For some years she had suffered ill health and my father, who adored her, worried about her continually, especially when he was so far away.

We did not go to London for Christmas 1943. On December 21st that year Nanny Hill died. By the time my father heard about her final illness she was already dead. My mother went to Brighton to be with Mabel and give her all the comfort and help that she could, while David and I stayed on the Garn with Nan and Granch, unaware of our parents' loss and sadness.

29-12-43

Your A.L. card of Dec. 15th arrived yesterday and the news about Mother is very bad…. The fact that both lungs are congested tells me that Mother is having a big fight to pull through. Your words are very comforting to me darling and I can only hope that the next letter will contain much happier news.

Sadly, it was not to be and in January 1944 he wrote:

I have just received Jack's letter telling me of Mother's passing on Dec. 21st.
[Jack Collins was Mabel's husband] When I received your letter last week telling me how ill Mother was, although I did not know it, she had already passed away.
I wanted so much for her to live until I came back and my sorrow is all the greater in knowing I could not be with her at the end. Mother fought so hard in every illness she had, and I remember when I

was called home to her when first in the Army how she smiled up at me and I told her she would pull through. I know how Mother worried about me; that, and the war, has accelerated her death I am sure.

I am finding consolation in knowing you are thinking of me and with me in my sorrow. I am thinking how hard it must be for Mabs and I know she did everything she could for Mother, so tell her I am grateful and always will be to her for taking on her burdens with such fortitude and giving Mother all the care she could. Mabs said you were the greatest comfort to her during that awful week and she does not know what she would have done without you.

3-1-44

I have just finished your A. L. Card and also a letter to Mabs. I wish I could come home darling to be with you all and I am praying that Jack's efforts on my behalf will prove successful. I know how you would have wished me home, not only for yourself but for me to have been with Mother before the end. It is so hard knowing my face cannot betray the sadness and ache in my heart for I have my job to carry on. Yet I know you have been sharing my sorrow. I had a premonition something was wrong a few days before Xmas, call it intuition if you like but I had a feeling something was wrong about Mother. I have been uneasy ever since her fall a few weeks back as her waning strength could not cope with even a slight accident.

There will be several things to straighten out and may the efforts that end to get me home be soon. I believe if you try hard enough I could get home to settle up Mother's affairs but it must be done from that end before I can know anything here. You know sweet I used to see to all Mother's affairs and there are some things even Mabs, Bill and Gus know nothing of. Mother signed a lot of policies and documents over to me when she was so ill soon after we were married and if I remember rightly nothing was ever touched or changed.

I want to know if Mother was buried with Dad and I want a memorial stone for both of them. There is so much passing through my brain at the moment I cannot quite sort things out. I am having a fairly hard time of it and the weather is mostly wet and cold. There is one thing I did not write to Mother about and that was my North Africa Star and Eighth Army Clasp, but I know she would have been very proud of me. Well my love I am longing to have your next letter and I hope it contains news about my getting home. Tell Mabs, Bill and Gus my thoughts were with them when I knew. Give my Nibs a big hug for me sweet and all my love to you darling.

9-1-44

Its been a long lonely week since the last letter I had but today I had two letters from you, the one you wrote on Xmas day and the one of Dec. 29th, telling me about the funeral. I gather from your letter that my brothers wanted to settle things up even before dear Mother was buried. For my part, I wish nothing material of Mother's, all I want is to treasure the joy of loving memories a boy has for his Mother. You alone sweet will have known how I felt when I received the news, for I was alone amongst men as I have been for many long weary months. I wanted to turn to someone but you were there with me as you have been in all my trials and tribulations. Your love and understanding has been my greatest treasure at all times. What I owe to you can only be repaid by my homecoming.........

The War Office did not let me know about Mother, and I have heard nothing about Jack's effort to get me home, so I take it his effort was of no avail....

These must have been some of the darkest and loneliest weeks for my father of his five-year Army career.

Nanny Hill 1942.

54

Chapter Nine
London 1944

Our second memorable Christmas visit to London was in 1944, after we had returned to Hove. My Father had now been fighting in the Middle East for almost two and a half years but my parents' love for each other never faltered and they existed on their letters, always believing that the war would soon end and they and their children would be together again. My Father kept up a vast correspondence with many of his family and friends and wrote to my Mother very frequently, sometimes twice a day. She kept about four hundred of these letters which give some insight to the heartache and longing, and unceasing worry that the worst could happen at any time.

The Solleys had moved from Hammersmith and, to our great delight, had taken on a sweet shop and general stores in Hornsey. Christmas was coming and a fat goose was just what Aunty Solley managed to procure in order to feed a great gathering of family and friends. One of the mysteries of the war years was her ability to come by luxuries that few could obtain, but she always shared such bounty generously with her friends. In addition to her other talents, she was a superb cook whose natural vocation in life was the dispensing of lavish hospitality.

Charlie had asked if he could bring his latest girlfriend, Stella (aptly named for she sparkled like a star), to join the festivities. He had brought her home a few times and I thought she was the prettiest girl I had ever seen, so I looked forward to meeting her again. On Christmas Eve Charlie had an important job to do. An ice-cream making machine, the old-fashioned kind which required hours of churning by hand, came with the shop. Charlie and his two male cousins set about their mammoth task, packing the outer bucket with ice and salt while the inner container was filled with ice-cream mixture. It was extremely laborious work, turning the handle against the resistant force of the packed ice, and the young men took it in turns till they were fairly exhausted. Aunty Solley and Mam were deep in food preparations, Uncle Charles was hidden away putting the finishing touches to his special gifts, and any spare hands were busy decorating the Christmas tree and pandering to its insatiable demand for piles of presents, wrapped and labelled, to be placed beneath its branches.

Charlie had finished making the ice-cream and became aware of the mounting parcels around the tree. The name *'Stella'* stared out at him from many labels. *'Oh, by the way,'* he remarked casually, *'I'll be bringing Rita along tomorrow, not Stella.'*

Aunty Solley eyed him for a few seconds to make sure he wasn't kidding, then ticked him off, half playfully, *'Well why didn't you tell us before, you young scoundrel? I'll knock your block off one of these days!'* Charlie soon charmed his way back into his mother's heart, reminding her she had met Rita before and liked her. There was just one tiresome problem, however. All of Stella's presents now became Rita's, and all the labels had to be changed!

The children were eventually removed from all this feverish activity and put to bed but not before they had hung up their stockings and knelt to say their prayers. Looking back, I can quite see why David was such a favourite with everyone, he not only kept them amused with his hilarious sayings and antics, but he had the virtue of knowing what a bed was for and could close his eyes and fall asleep almost immediately, whereas I often stayed awake for hours, especially when excitement was insurmountable, as on Christmas Eve. The more tightly I closed my eyes, the brighter the images which danced before them - pictures of presents, and parties and people jostled for space in my head, chasing each other around while I tossed and turned and grew, it seemed, more wide awake. Blissful sleep must have eventually stolen upon me, however, for in the morning my stocking was bulging with good things from Father Christmas. In the top there were always a few small presents: new hair slides, a pair of socks, a puzzle game; next a few chocolates and sweets; then the fruits, my arm stretching farther down the stocking for each one to reveal an apple, an orange and perhaps even a tangerine; then the nuts, and right in the toe a shiny new half-crown. Two very excited children then awoke the whole household.

Although we were Baptists in Wales we became Anglicans in London, and were amused at all the standing up and kneeling down that was required in church, but the traditional carols were familiar enough and we sang heartily. There had been some anxiety before we departed over the low pressure of the gas. Would the goose be thoroughly cooked? Aunty Solley wisely decided, on this of all days, to trust in Providence. Christmas Dinner was late but a feast fit for a royal household.

The ingredients for the Christmas pudding had been carefully hoarded throughout the year and when it arrived - flaming, black and crowned with holly - it was held high and greeted with cheers and applause. The over-rich and sticky mass was not a particular favourite with David and me at that age except in one respect. Hidden inside were silver threepenny bits wrapped in greaseproof paper, and we anticipated finding at least two each, while Uncle Charles would secretly slide a half-crown piece onto each of our plates, saying, *'Look what I found in your pudding!'* After the meal, we stood up when the National Anthem was played over the wireless, and then listened in solemn silence to the King's wartime broadcast.

Clearing away the remains of the feast and washing up the dishes came next. Then the moment arrived we had all been waiting for: the arrival of Father Christmas in his long red robe and hood trimmed with white fur, and his white beard and moustache. He made a little speech of greeting then handed out the presents one by one. It seemed a shame that Charlie had had to go on a mysterious errand just at this exciting time, but Father Christmas piled up his presents for him just by Rita and commented what a lucky chap he was. Rita was golden-haired and almost as pretty as Stella. After distributing all the presents, Father Christmas wished everyone a Merry Christmas and a Happy New Year, and then he disappeared. Very soon afterwards Charlie came back again, but David and I were too busy unwrapping a very large parcel addressed to both of us to attach any significance to this.

Inside the large parcel was a toy sweet shop, double-fronted with a recessed doorway, and a pitched roof painted red, while the windows displayed tiny jars of sweets filled with dolly mixtures, jelly babies and liquorice allsorts. The back of the shop could be opened up for small hands to gain access to the jars of sweets which they lost no time in doing. This marvellous toy had been lovingly made and painted by Uncle Charles, of course. Everyone was opening their presents and gasping in amazement at the things which had been procured in wartime austerity, and grateful for knitted garments during cold winters when central heating was unheard of amongst our class of people. Presents were carefully unwrapped (no ripping open) and the paper spread open and preserved for next year. At teatime there was ice-cream and jelly, crackers and party hats, mottos, jokes and riddles and plenty of noise and laughter. More guests arrived later for mince-pies and sherry, and the party continued into the small hours, but at some point two sleepy heads were laid down on pillows and drifted into sleep in spite of the sound of the grown-ups having a really good time.

Another huge party took place on New Year's Eve when we were all invited to the Mackies across the street to join in their traditional Hogmanay celebrations. As midnight began to strike, we all crossed arms and joined hands to sing Auld Lang Syne. Suddenly everyone stopped singing and went deadly quiet, listening to a sound which made the grown-ups go white with terror - the unmistakable drone of a Doodlebug overhead. The noise stopped and everyone held their breath. Moments later there was a terrific explosion, so close we felt the walls vibrating and thought the very roof was caving in over our heads. Mercifully, we were all unscathed, but a house a few doors away took the full force of the German bomb, and its occupants were all killed. My mother did not need much persuasion to return immediately to the comparative safety of Hove.

Chapter Ten
Return to Hove

All through those years of evacuation in Wales, my mother set her sights on eventual and permanent return to Hove. It was her mission. Throughout the correspondence there is a constant theme: Elsie's wish *'to go back home'*. Home, to her, now meant the little house she and my father had established in Hove, and she sacrificed other things in order to keep up the payments of rent. Many times, it seems, she was on the point of returning because *'the war may be over any time soon'*, and many times she was prevented by something, usually a renewed scare of heavy air raids, or the very real threat of an invasion, and most of all by my father's pleas that we should remain safely in Wales until his return. His return - it was remarkable how their mutual faith and optimism, and the loyalty and devotion so evident in the letters, kept up their strength during the unbearable years of separation, and the agony of not knowing when it would end - or how it would end. For many did not return, and many who did come back would never be whole in body and mind again.

David and I believed we had always lived in Wales but our mother kept alive in us an embryo memory of our former home and the people who lived round about, and our proximity to the sea. So there was a happy anticipation of meeting old friends, paddling in the sea, and most of all, having a father again. No doubt Pearl and Dolly who lived across the road and were fixed in my mind as little girls of my age, would have been amused to know I cast them in roles in several plays I had made up. They were now well on the way to being young women who would soon leave school and start work!

It was now 1944 and Britain and her allies were into their fifth year of war with Hitler's Germany and with Japan. Italy had been vanquished and had become an ally. There were encouraging signs that, with the help of the American forces, the allies would soon bring this terrible world-wide conflict to a swift and victorious conclusion. London, Coventry and other cities had suffered devastating bombing with many casualties, but the British Isles had resisted invasion by the enemy. Many families had received bad news: husbands, brothers, sons who had been taken prisoner or, worse still were missing, presumed dead, and would never return. The knock of the telegram boy was a sound to be feared. In sum, spirits were flagging, the vast majority of people were sick of the waste and carnage, and all looked towards generals and governments to bring the nightmare to an end, and restore our countries to some normality of life.

More optimistic news about the progress of the war must have prompted my mother to return to Hove on her own and to open up the house there in September 1944. Barbara Solley went down from London to stay with her and help bring the house to life again after its long slumbering emptiness. Babs wrote to Dad to say how thrilled she was to be helping Auntie Elsie, and this was reassuring to him. He was buoyed up with the hope of an early release, as the news suggested that older men with families were to be given priority. However, his hopes were cruelly dashed when he was suddenly told he had been *'selected'* to transfer to the Infantry. This was a dreadful blow to him after all his time in the Royal Artillery and he was not looking forward to the training. His letters from his new posting make heart-rending reading: *'It's going to be hard I know, but I've had some strange jobs and callings during my time in the Army and I've learned one thing, it's no use kicking against anything, but it's best to put one's back into it and get it done.'* He goes on to say he may now lose the rank of Sergeant which he's held for the past eighteen months and for which he worked so hard.

Soon after this letter he wrote to say he was in hospital with a knee injury.

Although I'd give lots not to be here, it's the nearest approach to Heaven I've known since leaving you my darling. I mean it's so wonderful to be in a real bed with a mattress, clean sheets and all the kindly attention one could wish for. I have not the faintest idea how long I shall be here. I can lie here, love, thinking of you all the time and know you will be thinking of me. It's something fresh for me to hear the wireless nearly all day long. We had Anne Shelton on today in her programme 'Anne to You'. Yesterday we listened to the football match England v. Scotland and the interest was very keen for there are a few Scots lads in our ward.

He was kept in the field hospital until 12th November and then transferred to a convalescent depot until the end of the year.

While my father was in hospital we were busy packing as many of our belongings as possible for the house was now ready for occupation. We hugged our goodbyes to grandparents, uncles and aunts, and waved tearfully from the Newport train that would now steam us back to Brighton and a new era of our lives. It seemed that Granch wanted to keep David on the Garn with them for a while but Dad wrote: *'I know how much he would like to keep David up at the Garn, but I think as you do that he still needs a mother's attention and guidance.'*

Aunty Glad wrote to Dad to say how they would all miss us as *'three and a half years is a long time to be with someone.'*

One of our first treats was a bus ride from Brighton to Hove along Western Road. Every time the bus passed a street with a clear view down to the seafront, David and I shouted excitedly, *'I can see the sea!'* until my mother's embarrassment forced

A group of Royal Artillery soldiers in Middle East, Father 2nd left, back row.

Elvina, with David on Ferdinand the Bull.

her to stop us shouting, so then we whispered it to each other. However, it was to be a long while before we could get close to the sea and the beach. Access was barred along the whole length of that coast by rolls of barbed wire, both to forestall an attempt at an invasion and to protect the public from mines.

Exploring the house and garden we had seen once, perhaps twice, on brief visits with Mam during the war, was very exciting. Discovering toys too bulky to transport to Wales such as the dolls' house and Ferdinand the Bull (he was our rocking bull instead of a rocking horse) was also fun. Ferdinand's working parts were oiled and then we were away, making up for the missed years of riding him. Although it was dusk, I ran out into the street and grabbed the first child I saw: a rough little urchin with bright red hair and brought her in to have a go on Ferdinand - and my did she ride him! She thought she was Roy Rogers in a Western until she went flying right over Ferdinand's head and fortunately landed on the settee. My mother then suggested that it would be a good idea if she went home - straight away - in her no-nonsense voice. And the little Irish tough-nut ran off.

The following day I got to know her whole family: her two older brothers, Ronnie and Michael, and her elder sister Maureen who was such a contrast - poised and feminine - and their dear little sister Sheena, a waif of four or five who was unable to speak clearly. Sheena was very pretty, though rather scrawny and sharp-featured like her mother and Ronnie. She grabbed hold of my hand and refused to let go, and after that, whenever she saw me, she would hold onto me all the time in an affectionate way so I could never shrug her off even if it was sometimes inconvenient. It transpired that Sheena was somewhat deaf which accounted for her speech defects, and not feeble-minded as some people had supposed.

One weekend I organised races on a nearby green for all the neighbouring children who wished to join in and (much to my mother's dismay) gave away several of my story books as prizes. Mrs Murphy was so delighted with the books her children won that she gave me a present - a small leather case containing a small flat-shaped clothes brush. On the case in gold letters was printed *'A handy brush for they who rush'*. I not only treasured this gift (because I am sure it was one of the few good possessions that Mrs Murphy owned) but found it very useful as a travelling companion. I kept it until 1992 when sadly it was stolen along with many other treasures from our house in Leicester.

Not long after our return, David and I were playing in the front garden when a big man came riding by on a bicycle. He stopped and demanded, *'Why aren't you children in school?'* He knocked loudly at the front door. *'Do these two children belong to you, madam?'* he demanded of our mother in a surly manner. *'Yes, why do you ask?'*

'Is there any legitimate reason why they are not attending school?'

'Well, we have only just returned from evacuation in Wales and there have been far too many things for me to sort out to even think about schools.'

'You had better start thinking about them right away,' said the School Bobby (or Truant Officer), *'or I shall have to report them as playing truant.'*

This idea shocked our mother. She knew she would have to enrol us into the local school but it had not been her first priority. The following day we were taken to Portland Road Infants School and settled into our new classrooms. Making friends took longer.

'Don't you talk funny,' they said in their Sussex brogue. *'Say some fink, go on, say some fink!'*

'*No*,' I said in my Welsh accent and they all laughed their heads off. David and I very soon learned the local lingo in order to be accepted. However, my first teacher liked my way of pronouncing every syllable when I was asked to read aloud, and all the class had to repeat after me '*strawberry jam*' and not '*strawbry*' which was the local way. Life was going to need a fine balancing act at the age of seven between pleasing my teachers and making friends.

After Christmas I was put up into the top class where I found the work much harder and I was up against some quite talented children in a mixed class. Two boys in particular excelled in drawing and painting - my weakest subject. One day, Miss Williams was so shocked at my pathetic efforts she held up my drawing to the rest of the class as an example of a very bad piece of work. Then she pushed up my sleeve and slapped my bare arm until it was as red as her hair. This was the only time I was ever physically punished at school. Strangely, it didn't improve my drawing ability.

At the age of eight we were moved across to the Junior School building on the other side of the playground. Here, boys and girls were in separate classrooms with the girls occupying one half of the school with a headmistress in charge, and the boys the other half under a headmaster. There were two streams in each of the three years, Class One being the top class, and Class Two those of the same age but lower ability, and so on down to Classes Five and Six at the bottom. There were at least forty pupils in each class sitting at double desks with the bench seat of the one in front attached to the back of the one behind. When you opened your desk lid it was empty underneath except for a narrow tray in which you could place a few personal items such as a snack for playtime, or a ball or skipping rope to play with. The desks had inkwells and a ridge near the top for holding pens and pencils. Each Monday morning the inkwells were carefully filled from a can by the ink monitor and a small piece of new pink blotting paper was issued to each pupil.

The large blackboard stood on an easel with a narrow shelf for holding chalks and a duster. It was considered quite a privilege to do small jobs to help teacher, and we had monitors for collecting and returning the register to the office; inkwell and blotting paper monitors; and several monitors for collecting in and handing out marked exercise books. When the blackboard needed cleaning hands shot up to perform that dusty operation, but only the tallest with the longest arms were chosen.

One day when I was particularly bored by a lesson, I decided to practise sneezing to see how realistic I could make it sound. I obviously did not succeed very well for Miss Rudd (we liked to pretend her name was Miss Rude) suddenly snapped, *'Elvina Hill, go and stand behind the blackboard!'*

Our school day was much longer than it is for pupils now. We had to arrive at 8.30 a.m. and were not allowed home until 4.00 p.m. But we had a recess for playtime in the afternoon as well as the morning. It may not be a coincidence that the vast majority of pupils left school in those days able to read and write, in spite of larger classes. Well, that was my impression. Also, the strict application of the law concerning school attendance, reinforced by the martinet school bobby, meant truancy was less of a problem.

Outbreaks of dreaded lice infestations were also fewer since we were regularly inspected by the school nurse. This was always considered a welcome break from lessons when we queued up in the corridor, the reek of Dettol growing stronger as one neared the medical room. When it was your turn, in you went, the comb was dipped in the disinfectant solution, and your hair parted and examined for evidence of lice and nits. Fortunately, my brother and I never suffered from this nasty infestation which was then considered only to attack those who were lax about personal hygiene. Boys invariably had the hair-style known as 'short back and sides', and girls either had short hair or plaits which may have hampered the little critters.

Making up plays and dressing up was what I enjoyed most in my spare time. Barbara Solley (who was nine years older than I) was a great encourager and provider of dressing-up clothes. She handed on two velvet capes, one blue, one red, and a splendid patriotic dance dress in red, white and blue satin, with gold-fringed epaulettes. There were also other dresses, fur stoles, a cloak edged with *'ermine'* and useful pieces of colourful material. For our *'Always England'* show I found a piece of red, white and blue material which was only large enough to make one pair of pants for one girl. So I went to Aunty Grace, my godmother, for help. She found another piece of material in plain dark red and suggested we could have two matching pairs of pants if we made them using the Union Jack material for the front and the plain material for the back. Then she helped me to cut them out and machine them.

We all knew the words to the popular patriotic songs of the time and practised them along with some choreographic imitations of dance routines we had seen in films and locally on the stage, and which always included linking arms at shoulder height with high leg-kicking. Sometimes we persuaded our mothers to come along and watch. Chairs were placed on our back lawn for the audience, and I persuaded my mother to provide jam tarts (her speciality) and cups of tea for everyone during the interval. The interval was necessary for the actors, as changing costumes as often as possible was the greatest fun and most important aspect of the staging since we had no scenery apart from the odd chair, table and stool.

There was great jubilation when V.E. Day (Victory in Europe) was declared on the 8th of May 1945 and many street parties were planned, including ours. An elderly and much respected gentleman who lived behind a high privet hedge at the bottom of the road was invited to become Chairman of the Street Party Committee. My mother was part of the organising committee along with several others, and they planned who was going to make the cakes, sandwiches and jellies, and who was going to provide the pots of tea and lemonade. Apparently, some places managed to have impromptu parties right away but most were held between mid-May and June.

No one in our street owned a car except the taxi-driver opposite so there were no hazards in setting trestle tables down the middle (where they came from remains a mystery). Sheets made good substitute table-cloths and they were decorated with red, white and blue streamers and patriotic bunting was strung between lamp-posts. Delicious food appeared as if by magic (people must have been saving their rations for weeks). Such bounty: plates piled high with sandwiches, cakes (even iced ones), jam tarts, buns and biscuits. Oh, the wonderful gluttony of it all, the tremendous release of fear and oppression! There were wireless broadcasts and newsreels of the crowds in Trafalgar Square, and pictures in the newspapers of the Royal Family on the balcony of Buckingham Palace waving to the cheering crowds. All these things didn't happen at once on the same day, but memory crowds them together in a crescendo of tumultuous common joy. There is the iconic photograph in Picture Post of the unknown sailor kissing the unknown girl in Trafalgar Square which perfectly sums up the mood of the nation.

When the paraphernalia of the street party had been cleared away, many of us went down to the seafront to watch the fireworks. For the first time since war began a band was playing on the bandstand on Hove seafront with everyone dancing, and members of the armed forces in their uniforms throwing coins around for the children who went scrabbling amongst the feet of the dancing couples. It was an overwhelming experience. Finally, as the band struck up the National Anthem, everyone respectfully stood still until the last note died away. Then we clapped and cheered and our mother grabbed David and me by the hand and we followed the streaming crowds up the streets and home to bed.

There was only one thing missing for many of us to fill our cup to overflowing - the long-awaited return of fathers, husbands, brothers, sisters. Surely, now, the government would waste no time in bringing the forces home - those who had been fortunate enough to come through it all - to a glorious reunion with their families. Alas, it did not happen right away. The government could not have misjudged the sense of urgency and anticipation in the nation, but they must have had their reasons for the delay - political, logistical, compromise - demobilisation was not going to happen overnight.

As I mentioned earlier, my father was one of those 'selected' to be transferred to the Infantry, the 2nd Battalion Sherwood Foresters, and sent to Syria to quell a fomenting uprising there. The hard training he would be forced to undergo for this final momentous task after three and a half years' active service in the desert almost certainly severely undermined his health. It was a punishing regime which he bravely bore because, as he said, it was no use kicking against the army, the best way was head down and get on with it. It is heart-breaking to read his letters of the agonising wait for release. The lack of information, the rumours and resentment circulating amongst the men, made a troublesome time for them all. But there were some compensations.

Letter 7-4-45 (Extract)

…I have been busy for several weeks on an N.C.O's course, and as a special treat a trip to the Holy City was arranged for us. The fact that our Padre conducted the tour made it something so wonderful I shall never forget. We visited Bethlehem first and just before we arrived I saw the hills of Judea which surround Jerusalem, Nazareth and Bethlehem. I cannot express the true beauteous wonder of all I saw.

After seeing the place where the Manger lay, we went to the spot where the Three Wise Men from the east laid their presents at the feet of Christ. Not more than a hundred yards from there I went into a shop and bought you a real mother-of-pearl necklace hung with a crucifix bearing an image of Christ in silver to mark the occasion.

I know how your thoughts must dwell on my homecoming. I keep hoping the news will be the news we are all waiting for….

Just a month later his wishes came true.

7-5-45 (Extract)

I heard five minutes ago sweetheart that the War is over in Europe. I hope it's true but in any case I had made up my mind that the moment I heard the news we have all so long awaited I would write to you, as my first thoughts were of you and my Nibs. Even though this is such joyous news and we will thank God that so many of us have been spared, I cannot help but think of those who have given their all, their lives, to make sure that we shall live in peace again. I think of my own pals and chums who will not be going home but who lie somewhere in the Desert, their job so magnificently done.

10-5-45 (Extract)

…. Received your letter May 2nd yesterday. Well my precious one we are now sure that the war in Europe is over……It must have been wonderful for people back home and from all the news I've heard on the radio, everyone went wild with delight…We had as good a time as could be expected for we held our celebrations in camp. On the Tuesday we did not have reveille until 07/5 hours, breakfast at eight o'clock. Then we had Thanksgiving Service. Afterwards my own Company decided to take our lunch to the seaside, which is about half an hour's run away by truck. I had a swim and we all made merry, although at that time we only had lemonade to drink

We came back in time to hear Mr Churchill's speech. In the evening we had a concert and singsong and there was lots of beer to drink. The next day we were allowed to stay in bed until eight o'clock and had breakfast at nine. We arranged our own fun fair and had lots of side-shows. Then we had a race meeting with mules, donkeys and camels. The race meeting was great fun and I rode in some of the races. Then in the evening we had another singsong and more beer.

Well darling you see we made the most of it, but you were missing and my real Victory Day will be when I come home again. This is all for now my angel. God bless you all.

Your ever loving and devoted husband, Vin.

Vin and Elsie at Barry Island.

Chapter Eleven
Homecoming

By September 1945 when I went up to the Juniors, we had been back in Hove for a year and were thoroughly immersed in games with friends and playing out in the street until the lamp-lighter came round on his bicycle, stopping at each lamp to switch it on with his long pole. He came round again in the small hours to switch the lamps off, and performed an extra service to the community by knocking with his long pole on the bedroom windows of those who had to get up very early for work. Each lamp-post had a bar about a foot in length which stuck out at right angles just beneath the lamp, and boys would climb up and swing on the bar before jumping down into the road. My seven year old brother was no exception and he also joined a gang of mostly older boys that went off to play on bomb sites.

One night he stayed out until nightfall and Mum left me alone in the house for what seemed an eternity while she went searching for him. Eventually she returned with her adventurous wayward lad, and said bomb sites were now out of bounds. However, we were still allowed great freedom to roam in the daytime with our friends to Wish Road Park and Portslade Recreation Ground.

Christmas was not far off and the troops were gradually arriving back in Britain to the welcome of the nation and the longed-for reunions with their families. I can vividly remember the night when my father came home from the war. It was about 11 o'clock one December night. I was eight years old, in bed, but tossing and turning, unable to sleep. I was startled by a loud knock at the front door and I knew at once it was my Daddy coming home. The door was opened and I heard, *'My Darling Elsie,' 'My Darling Vin,'* then the sounds of hugs, kisses and tears. After a while I heard my Father say eagerly, *'Can I see the children?' 'Well David will be asleep,'* said my mother, *'but I know Elvina will still be awake.'*

And what a homecoming it was! His huge army kit-bag was bulging with presents and toys and strange-looking Palestinian sweets. There was a donkey for David and a camel for me, both made of leather; beautiful delicate Palestinian silver jewellery; exotic satin pyjamas and matching house-coat for Mum; a decorative ivory crucifix with a tiny spy-hole of glass which, when you looked through it, revealed a picture of the Holy Land, and many more wonderful surprises. Then as we played with our new toys and munched the bags and bags of sweets, he told us fascinating stories of the many countries through which he had travelled, holding us spellbound for hours.

That was the only Christmas he was ever able to spend at home with his family because he had been given extended leave before starting work again. From then on we sacrificed his company every Christmas so that he could provide the most wonderful festive occasion for the guests at the hotel where he worked. He was a perfectionist who worked far too hard, but everyone adored him. A bonus, however, was that some days he would be there in the afternoons when we came home from school. These were days when he was not *'on teas'* and could take a couple of hours' break before returning to supervise dinner for the guests.

In spite of working such long hours (7.30 a.m. to 9 p.m.), he still managed to spend time with us and take us out. He always had a fund of antics and jokes to keep us amused, and would perform various impromptu tricks such as spinning a tray around poised on one finger, and then with one glass on the tray, and once he took a tray full of items and spun them around but they all went crashing to the floor, and after that Mum banned tray-spinning for quite a while. He also practised the trick of pulling a table-cloth off the table and leaving the items still in place - occasionally with the same dire results. But he had such charming ways and so loved to entertain that his wife could not be cross with him for long. Best of all, we were a complete family again and quite settled back into life in Hove though we always looked forward to returning to Wales for several weeks every summer holiday.

Many friends and relations came from Wales to stay with us for a seaside holiday. My mother was a born cook and hostess and she loved entertaining visitors, so the house was often full to overflowing in the summer. Looking back, I cannot imagine where we all slept, but wartime conditions had inured us to somewhat cramped conditions and mostly we enjoyed their company. There was one strange boy, however, who perplexed us, the son of a Blaenavon councillor who was second cousin to Mum. He found an old suitcase mouldering in the garden shed and spent his time collecting snails and keeping them in the suitcase. One day, he opened the case to show David and me his collection, and I found it a revolting sight - dozens of snails with their horns extended crawling around leaving moist trails. He would have been a valuable asset to any gardener.

During the summer of 1946 I noticed that our slender mother was beginning to look fatter, but it did not particularly strike me until November 5th. David and I begged her to take us to a bonfire party nearby and she walked so slowly I thought it would all be over by the time we arrived. *'She's getting far too fat,'* I muttered to David. A few days after Guy Fawkes' night we were told to pack our school clothes, nightwear, toilet bags, plimsoll bags and books, and were taken up to Aunty Grace's house. *'Mummy has to go into hospital,'* said Daddy, *'as she is going to have a baby, a little brother or sister for you.'* This was quite a shock but we were excited by the idea.

On November 11th 1946 my little sister was born at the Buckingham Road Nursing Home by Caesarian section, as were David and I. She was born on Nanny Hill's birthday, the eleventh day of the eleventh month, and was the eleventh grandchild on both sides of the family. It was a Sunday morning and Aunty Grace switched on the wireless to listen to the broadcast from the Cenotaph in London where the King was laying a wreath. As eleven o'clock struck for the two-minute silence, Aunty Grace told David and her son Ian it was a five-minute silence so we could have some peace and quiet from their continual noise.

Every morning I would be washed and dressed long before the boys so I could go downstairs and enjoy an early-morning cup of tea with Aunty Grace - we called it *'Ours on the Quiet'* (O.O.T.Q.). I loved the special relationship I had with my godmother. She was very good to us and every morning she placed an apple in each of our school bags to eat at playtime which was a great treat. There were three single beds in the large back bedroom which I had to share with the two boys. As I have already mentioned, I found it hard to get off to sleep, so when the boys were asleep, I would switch the light back on again (it didn't seem to disturb them as their beds were in an alcove away from the light) and read a book - often one of Ian's collection of Just William stories. One night, about midnight, Uncle Jack opened the door, switched off the light without a word and closed the door again. The following night I smuggled a torch up to bed with me and continued to read under the covers.

Mum was kept in the nursing home for three weeks and we were not allowed to visit her so the homecoming was very exciting for us and we both adored out baby sister - until she got old enough to be annoying! It was a bitterly cold winter with temperatures often well below freezing, and sometimes we were sent home from school because the outside lavatories were frozen. There were many shortages of food and fuel, especially coal which everyone depended on for heating their homes. It must have been particularly hard for mothers with babies to care for. I can well remember the huge fender round the fireplace with all the nappies drying on it, denying us the warmth we craved. Our one modern convenience was an immersion heater but that had to be used sparingly. Gas and electricity were paid for by feeding shilling coins into their respective meters and sometimes there were none to spare. When the light went out suddenly, there was a cry of *'Who's got a shilling for the meter?'* at the same time as grabbing a torch or even lighting a match. Sometimes, in fact quite often, the light went out because there was a power cut.

Families of today may have their problems, but they have no idea of the privations suffered by the majority of the populace during the war and the first few years afterwards until the country got back on its feet. Food and clothes were still on ration. Shops invariably had queues stretching along the pavement, especially if news went round like wildfire that there had been a delivery of some exotic food item such as bananas or oranges. Every Saturday morning, David and I were sent to queue up at Nightingales the Bakers opposite our school. Our order was always for two large square sandwich loaves.

One week Mum said we could buy a Madeira cake as well and gave us the extra money. Aunty Solley and Babs (now living in Hove again) were invited to tea that day and we were all looking forward to a slice of cake. Mum cut two or three slices, and then we saw a date! Everyone clamoured for the slice with the date. But when she cut the cake again, the *'date'* was discovered to have legs attached! In fact it was a huge black beetle - so no one was allowed any cake at all. And on Monday morning the cake went back to Nightingales'.

Scarcity of basic food items meant rationing was even stricter than during the war. People were definitely slimmer then - as revealed by any documentaries and newsreels of the 1940's and 50's. Very few people were even fat, let alone obese. Hardly any ordinary families could afford the luxury of a car, and lack of money for bus fares made walking and cycling the main modes of transport.

Dad had one day off a week from St. Catherine's Lodge Hotel where he was employed as Assistant Head Waiter (originally, the allowance had been only half a day!), and this was Sunday. How we enjoyed our Sundays then! Cooking was one of his hobbies and a cooked Sunday breakfast was a treat we looked forward to all week. He also liked to experiment so he tried making crisps. These were not as thin as Smith's Crisps (which were once again becoming available in the shops, each bag with its little twist of blue waxed paper containing salt. It was a sad day when the crisps were automatically sprinkled with salt and the little blue packets disappeared) but we thought Hill's Crisps were scrumptious. A year later he was appointed Head Waiter and his day off was changed to Tuesday, so instead of cooking breakfast he made cakes for tea. His other hobbies, apart from acting the clown, were playing the banjo-ukelele, reading and horse-racing (as a spectator I hasten to add). He took banjo lessons by post and we would crowd round the piano while I plonked out the tune, playing by 'ear', and enjoy a great sing-song.

He enjoyed all kinds of sport - even boxing although he was the mildest-tempered and most peace-loving man, and he had played football and cricket on sand while in the desert. He told us our great-grandfather was renowned as a bare-fist fighter, so when David was taught boxing as one of the sports offered at his school, Dad was there coaching him. Likewise with football, and I was dragged along to the schoolboy matches on many a freezing cold Saturday.

David and I attended Sunday School at Stoneham Road Baptist Church. Boys and girls were in small separate classes in age groups. Any boy who misbehaved was sent to stand in one of the far corners of the platform with his back turned. Girls didn't misbehave - by definition - and strict order was kept by `young` Mr Sadler. First there were communal hymns, prayers and a Bible reading, after which we sat in a circle with our individual teachers. Miss Hopkins gave each of us a small decorated text every Sunday until my Bible was stuffed with them, and remains so to this day.

Sometimes `old` Mr Sadler addressed the school, a dear, elderly gentleman with a smiling face and benign air. I often wondered how `young` Mr Sadler, so fierce-looking, could be his son. Amongst the notices given at the beginning there was mention of the Girls' Guildry and the day and time of meetings. I was keen to join and persuaded Mum to take me to the hall one Thursday evening. *'You're sure it's Thursday?'* she said. I nodded vigorously. It was a good twenty-five minutes' walk, but when we arrived and poked our heads round the door - it was full of boys! What a disappointment! I had misheard after all; Girls' Guildry met on Tuesdays.

At the age of seven I was in the youngest group called *'Poppies'*. We wore bright poppy-coloured dresses with a green petal collar. At eight you advanced to the Speedwells - where comfort was not the first concern - we wore stiff white shirts with long sleeves, fiercesome cuffs, and starched collars, teamed with dark skirts and blue berets - and a speedwell badge. Miss Cole was the Commander and Miss Pugh was the Treasurer. They lived in a charming house in one of the best roads in Hove. One summer they held a garden party for the Guildry. When I arrived with some friends, the front door was opened by a maid straight out of Just William - black dress, white frilled apron and cap. She led us right through the house and into the vast garden which had a large summer-house at the far end where tea, sandwiches and cakes were being served.

Occasionally we had to take exams in scripture and embroidery. A scripture exam was held one December evening when snow was falling. When we boarded the charabanc (Miss Coles pronounced the word 'Sharabong') which was to take us to the exam venue we found a luxurious blanket on every seat to wrap round our legs to keep us warm. Scripture, of course, was a written exam. Our embroidered tray cloths were sent away for marking. When both lots of results came through I remember being cross that I had obtained higher marks for scripture for which (I'm ashamed to say) I had done no preparation, than for my embroidery over which I had taken great pains.

There was a small playground near the hall with swings, a see-saw and a roundabout. In the winter we had snowball fights there and continued them on the small green near home. This was exciting as the older boys joined in, some of them eighteen, until they began putting stones inside the snowballs which could really hurt if they hit you hard. Piles and piles of snow fell every winter of our first few years back in Hove. Lovely for the first week or so, then utter misery trudging through black slush, with sopping wet mittens, socks, scarves, hats - and chilblains.

There are two very sad memories I have connected with Sunday School. For a time I always went with my friend Winnie who lived a couple of doors away. Then she became ill and was in hospital for what seemed ages as she only went in to have her appendix taken out. When I next saw her I was shocked: she looked so thin and white but she came once more to Sunday School, and then went back into hospital and I never saw her again. Recently, looking through memorabilia, I came across a photo of Winnie aged nine looking wan and with a sad, sweet smile on her face, and that was how I remembered her, my lovely friend.

Winnie Shiers.

Living next door was another little girl I persuaded to come to Baptist Sunday School one week, but as the family was Roman Catholic she was never allowed to come again. Peggy had three brothers, the oldest of whom was Stanley aged fourteen, his mother's favourite. One day, Stanley was very late coming home from school so Mr Brooker who was a milkman and therefore finished work early, went to look for him while Mum and I kept Mrs Brooker company. His discovery was tragic: Stanley had suffered a heart attack and died on the way home. Mr Brooker returned alone. *'My dear,'* he said to his wife, *'I have some bad news - I'm afraid Stanley will never come home from school again.'*

I was nine when the beaches were cleared of barbed wire and that summer David and I learned to swim in the sea, taught by Charlie and Barbara Solley. It was magical being buoyed up by the salty water (though not when a wave hit you and you choked and spluttered). I couldn't wait till the following day to renew the experience. Mum was not keen on the beach as the sun gave her headaches. So in the summer holidays we often went down to the beach with a group of friends and stayed there all day long. About four o'clock Mum would come down to bring us some tea. She made superb sandwiches and she always wrapped them in a beautiful white damask linen napkin which was damp to keep them fresh. Then there was the welcome flask of hot tea. To sit on the beach wrapped in your towel after a swim, drinking tea, was heaven. Unless we had a heat wave there was usually a cool breeze blowing. The summer after Gloria was born Mum would push the pram down to the promenade and join us with the baby. It was easier in a way because she could stow the bags of food and drink underneath the pram.

For several years running, a gang of young children from our street would congregate on the beach together and there was never any trouble that I can remember. Just once, on a day when no parents had been able to join us, and we were all getting dried and dressed, did any strange adult interfere. A tall, odd-looking man whom I had noticed watching us for a while came up, and on the pretext of being kind and helpful, began advising us in a prurient way how to dry ourselves properly. None of us spoke to him, we tried to ignore him, and we all got dressed in sullen silence and moved off as quickly as possible as he gave us the creeps.

Sometimes we went to the Lagoon at the western end of Hove promenade where there

David and Elvina, Brighton boating lake, 1945.

was a shallow paddling pool and a large boating lake. We also explored the lawns, bowling greens and tennis courts situated between the coast road and the promenade. We scaled the high walls shoring up the promenade by clinging with the ends of our fingers to the extremely narrow ledges strengthening the walls. (There was always some means of adventure.) Another great attraction was a boating lake near the Palace Pier but this necessitated adult supervision.

Aunty Solley took on a variety of posts as housekeeper on her return to Sussex and wherever she went I was sure to be invited. When I was nine she became live-in housekeeper and child-minder to a widower who had a small-holding at Chiddingly and I went to stay with the family at Easter, sharing a room with fourteen-year old Valerie who had two younger brothers, Philip and Nicholas. Valerie decided to educate me on the facts of life and told me how a baby was created. I remember being very indignant and remonstrating with her: *'My mother would never do anything like that!'* So she took me to visit her rabbits for a demonstration.

Pleasanter memories float into view of long cycle rides down country lanes filling our cycle baskets with daffodils from the woods - a practice that is now frowned upon - and going shopping in Hailsham in Mr Pilbeam's large saloon car with the boys constantly fighting. I must have stayed at Christmas time as well for I remember Aunty Solley making chocolate truffles and rolling them in cocoa as one of the festive treats.

Another position she held was in a large detached house on Hove seafront where she was given a self-contained spacious flat in the basement. I stayed there a couple of times but could hardly sleep at night since I was given the put-you-up settee in the sitting-room which was in its own corridor off the main hallway. Not only did I think someone might come up that dark corridor in the

Aunty Solley, Charlie, Babs, Daddy, Frank, the Nibs 1946.

night to get me, I also feared the heavy back of the settee which was raised when the bed was pulled out might suddenly fall on my head. Later on, when I read James Thurber's Carnival, I identified with the character in the story of *'The night the bed fell'*. But all these fears were laid to rest in the day-time when I wallowed in Aunty Solley's spoiling. When the family was away she took me on a tour of the house and I was shocked by the state of the grown-up son's bedroom. *'Oh, he always throws all his dirty clothes on the floor for me to gather up,'* said Aunty.

Looking back, it would seem there were many and variable treats in those times of austerity, but also times of childhood illnesses. When I was seven I went into hospital to have my tonsils removed. Children were not allowed visitors then (in case it upset them and made life difficult for the nurses, I understand), so when I came home my mother cried as she hugged me. Poor David, however, did not receive any sympathy when he was suffering from chicken-pox. He was not keen on school, so when he said he felt unwell and had a headache and didn't want to go to school my mother said, *'You'll go to school if I have to beat you all the way.'* Of course, she didn't literally mean she would beat him, it was her colourful way of putting over a point. A few days later telltale spots appeared on the back of David's neck and our mother felt guilty for forcing him to attend school when he was not well. As he was probably still infectious she took him to Wales with her and left my father looking after me.

Unsurprisingly, I began to show symptoms of being unwell. Daddy kept me in bed and brought me dainty morsels of food to tempt me to eat, such as exquisitely prepared tiny triangular sandwiches. When the chicken-pox spots came out all over me he sent for the doctor who came and told him I couldn't go to school for three weeks nor play with other children. He sent an S.O.S. to Elsie to return from Wales as Elvina needed her. Being pampered when you feel ill is fine, but being confined to your own home and garden when you feel better but are still deemed infectious is boring. I wanted to be out playing in the street with my friends. In order to placate me, Mum put a little chair by the front door so I could watch the others at play. No sooner was her back turned than I skipped down the front garden path to join them, and it was some time before she discovered my disobedience.

Summer or winter we thrived on our street games and stayed out until dark, ignoring calls to *'Come in now,'* and then, *'Come in at once!'* As we got older and stayed out later we began to spy on courting couples, as they were then coyly known, and giggle as they kissed *'goodnight'*, little dreaming that before long we would be joining them in these strange activities.

* * *

In the summer of 1947, when baby Gloria was eight months old, we returned to Wales for our usual holiday with Nan and Granch. Kay Slope and Garn Drift collieries were still busy undermining the health of the miners, and the second slag heap was almost as high as the first. There was still squelching grass underfoot when you ventured off the path, with frogs leaping amongst the rushes; still plenty of straggly sheep and wild ponies roaming around; still the fresh, intoxicating mountain air working its magic. We ran, we leapt, we pranced and gambolled like the lambs in spring with boundless energy, up beside the brook to the spout and back again, then round and round Grancher's top field. We felt we wanted to hug the very earth from which the cottages rose up so naturally, nestling in their hollow. This was our homeland. Watching over the village, the magnificent Coity reigned supreme.

Invitations had come flooding in, Nan said, even before we had arrived: tea with Aunty Doll, tea with Aunty Glad, tea with Aunty Mary, tea with every real and adopted aunt for miles around. Pat Young and I slid naturally into our former friendship and spent much time together. Apart from the endless visiting, we made trips to Pontypool, Abergavenny, Ebbw Vale, Newport - and Hereford, our favourite outing.

As the summer wore on the sun ripened the whimberries on the Coity. Would they be blackest black and ripe enough to gather before our return to Hove? We awaited the verdict, keyed up with hope. Hooray! An expedition was arranged one Saturday, providing the weather was fine. And it was. On a bright sunny day a crowd set out with their baskets and climbed the Coity, frightening the scraggy sheep which were grazing on the sparse grass of the mountainside so they leapt nimbly away on their thin legs. The party scattered far and wide to find the choicest fattest berries. When the baskets were brimming, the bent bodies gradually stood upright, only then noticing how their backs were aching. Then they all descended, chattering and comparing baskets, eager to wash the fruit, remove stalks, and make the incomparable whimberry tarts for tea. The following morning I was awake very early.

The Coity lay slumbering, majestical, the ancient guardian of the valley, its lineage stretching back to time immemorial, its long, dark, whalian shape just visible against the sky. I had seen it in many different moods and guises; watched it change its shape and colour a thousand times, thrilled to its performance in all winds and weathers. Happiest when scudding clouds made running patterns of light and shade over its surface, most mysterious when shrouded in thick descending mist. Most threatening and dramatic when besieged by Thor's black skies, split in two by flashes of lightning and crashes of thunder while the gods unleashed a wall of water. Most harmonious with the valley, and smiling, when the day dawned mild and sunny.

And such a day was this, rich with my Grandfather's promise. Today we would climb the Coity together. We would take it slowly, at our leisure, stopping often to admire the views; sit for a while here and there, on a rock amidst the heather. As we mounted higher and higher the steepening climb made us pause for breath as the summit, teasing us like an Olympian God, moved further and further away. Would we ever reach the top? Renewing our energy with chocolate bars, we soldiered on towards our goal. At last the top, and suddenly before us stretched a wide plateau, and beyond another country with other mountain ranges rising up from valleys just like ours, ravaged by man's greed for coal. One day it would all be mended, healed, restored to its former beauty, though not in Grancher's time. But we had climbed the Coity together. I took his walking stick, reached up, and I do believe I touched the sky.